William Shakespeare was born in Stratford-upon-Avon in April 1564, and his birth is traditionally celebrated on April 23. The facts of his life, known from surviving documents, are sparse. He was one of eight children born to John Shakespeare, a merchant of some standing in his community. William probably went to the King's New School in Stratford, but he had no university education. In November 1582, at the age of eighteen, he married Anne Hathaway, eight years his senior, who was pregnant with their first child, Susanna. She was born on May 26, 1583. Twins, a boy, Hamnet (who would die at age eleven), and a girl, Judith, were born in 1585. By 1592 Shakespeare had gone to London, working as an actor and already known as a playwright. A rival dramatist, Robert Greene, referred to him as "an upstart crow, beautified with our feathers." Shakespeare became a principal shareholder and playwright of the successful acting troupe, the Lord Chamberlain's Men (later, under James I, called the King's Men). In 1599 the Lord Chamberlain's Men built and occupied the Globe Theatre in Southwark near the Thames River. Here many of Shakespeare's plays were performed by the most famous actors of his time, including Richard Burbage, Will Kempe, and Robert Armin. In addition to his 37 plays, Shakespeare had a hand in others, including *Sir Thomas More* and *The Two Noble Kinsmen*, and he wrote poems, including *Venus and Adonis* and *The Rape of Lucrece*. His 154 sonnets were published, probably without his authorization, in 1609. In 1611 or 1612 he gave up his lodgings in London and devoted more and more of his time to retirement in Stratford, though he continued writing such plays as *The Tempest* and *Henry VIII* until about 1613. He died on April 23, 1616, and was buried in Holy Trinity Church, Stratford. No collected edition of his plays was published during his lifetime, but in 1623 two members of his acting company, John Heminges and Henry Condell, published the great collection now called the First Folio.

William Shakespeare

THE COMEDY OF ERRORS

Edited by
David Bevington
and
David Scott Kastan

BANTAM CLASSIC

THE COMEDY OF ERRORS
A Bantam Book / published by arrangement with Pearson Education, Inc.

PUBLISHING HISTORY
Scott, Foresman edition published January 1980
Bantam edition, with newly edited text and substantially revised, edited, and
amplified notes, introduction, and other materials / February 1988
Bantam reissue with updated notes, introduction, and
other materials / February 2006

Published by Bantam Dell
A Division of Random House, Inc.
New York, New York

All rights reserved
Copyright © 2004 by Pearson Education, Inc.
Cover art copyright © 1988 by Mark English
This edition copyright © 2006 by Bantam Books
Revisions and annotations to Shakespeare text and its footnotes and textual
notes, Shakespeare's Sources essay and notes for the source, and the
play introduction © 1988, 2006 by David Bevington
The Playhouse text © 1988 by David Bevington
The Comedy of Errors On Stage and On Screen, © 1988, 2006 by
David Bevington and David Scott Kastan
Memorable lines © 1988, 2006 by Bantam Books
Annotated bibliography © 1988, 2006 by David Scott Kastan and James Shapiro

Valuable advice on staging matters has been provided by Richard Hosley
Collations checked by Eric Rasmussen
Additional editorial assistance by Claire McEachern

Book design by Virginia Norey

Library of Congress Catalog Card Number: 87-24095

Bantam Books and the rooster colophon are
registered trademarks of Random House, Inc.

ISBN-10: 0-553-21291-5
ISBN-13: 978-0-553-21291-4

Printed in the United States of America
Published simultaneously in Canada
OPM   17 16 15 14 13 12 11 10 9 8

CONTENTS

INTRODUCTION

The Comedy of Errors is a superb illustration of Shakespeare's
"apprenticeship" in comedy. It is more imitative of classical
comedy, especially of Plautus, than is Shakespeare's mature work.
Its verbal humor, including the scatological jokes about breaking
wind, the bawdy jests about cuckolds' horns, and the overly in-
genuous banter (as in 2.2), is at times adolescent. The play
abounds in the farcical humor of physical abuse, so endearing
to children of all ages. It is perhaps the most uncomplicatedly
funny of all Shakespeare's plays. Yet the softening touches
of Shakespeare's maturity are unmistakably present as well.
Shakespeare frames his farce of mistaken identity with old
Egeon's tragicomic story of separation, threatened death, and
eventual reunion. He adds characters to his chief sources,
Plautus's Menaechmi and Amphitruo, in order to enhance the
love interest and to reconcile Plautus with English moral conventions. He touches upon themes of illusion, madness, and
revelry that are to figure prominently in A Midsummer Night's
Dream and in Twelfth Night, a later comedy of mistaken identity.
In these respects, The Comedy of Errors is both a fascinating pre-
lude to Shakespeare's later development and a rich achievement
in its own right. On stage, it has not attracted the greatest
Shakespearean actors, since it offers no complex or dominating
roles, but it has seldom failed to delight audiences.

We cannot be sure precisely how early the play was written.
A performance took place on December 28, 1594, at Gray's Inn,
one of the Inns of Court, before an unruly assembly of lawyers, law students, and their guests. This was probably not the
first performance, however. Topical allusions offer hints of an
earlier date. When Dromio of Syracuse speaks of France as
"armed and reverted, making war against her heir" (3.2.123–4),

he clearly is referring to the Catholic League's opposition to Henry of Navarre, who was the heir apparent to the French throne until 1593, when he became king. Another allusion, to Spain's sending "whole armadas of carracks" (lines 135–6), would possibly have lost its comic point soon after the Invincible Armada of 1588. The play's style, characterization, and imitative construction are all consistent with a date between 1589 and 1593.

Whatever the exact date, Shakespeare's youthful fascination with Plautus is manifest. Shakespeare's command of Latin, though sneered at by Ben Jonson, was undoubtedly good enough to have let him read Plautus with pleasure. He must have been drilled in Latin for years as a student in the town of Stratford-upon-Avon. Indeed, the influence of not only Plautus but also Ovid and Seneca (together with touches of Horace, Catullus, etc.) is a prominent feature of Shakespeare's early work, dramatic and nondramatic. Shakespeare may have consulted Plautus both in the original and in a contemporary translation, as was frequently his custom with non-English sources. From Renaissance Latin editions of Plautus, he apparently took the odd designation "Antipholis Sereptus" (i.e., "surreptus," snatched away), which appears in the Folio text in a stage direction at 2.1.0 to indicate the twin who was separated from his father. On the other hand, a translation of the *Menaechmi* by "W. W." (? William Warner), published in 1595, was registered in 1594 and might have been available earlier to Shakespeare in manuscript.

Plautus had much to offer Shakespeare and his fellow dramatists, especially in the way of tightly organized and complex plot construction. Native English drama of the sixteenth century tended to be episodic and panoramic in its design. Shakespeare's apprenticeship in neoclassical form can be seen in his precise observation of the unities of time and place—those unities which he openly disregarded in most of his later plays. At the play's beginning, Egeon is informed that he has until sundown to raise his ransom money, and the play then moves toward that point in time with periodic observations that it is now noon, now two o'clock, and so on. (At one point, time even seems to go backwards, but that is part of the illusion of madness.) The action is restricted to the city of Ephesus; events that have happened elsewhere, at an earlier time (such as the separation of the Antipholus family), are told to us by persons in the play, such as old Egeon. Although Shakespeare's company did not employ the sort of painted scenery drawn in perspective used by continental neoclassicists, with fixed locations for houses facing on a street, the original production of this play may nonetheless have used one stage "house" or door to represent the dwelling of Antipholus of Ephesus (the Phoenix) throughout the drama. The entire play can be staged as if all the action occurs in the vicinity of this single "house," with the Courtesan's establishment and abbey near at hand. Never again does Shakespeare utilize such a neoclassical stage.

These unities of time and place are mechanical matters, but they do also harmonize with a more essential unity of action. The story moves, as though in perfect accord with neoclassical five-act theory, from exposition and complication to climax, anagnoresis (discovery), and peripeteia (reversal of fortune). The brilliance of the plotting is decidedly Plautine. Shakespeare pushes to its limit the interweaving of comic misunderstandings only to unravel all these seemingly tightly woven knots with ease. Yet the imitation of Plautus, even in matters of construction, is by no means slavish, for Shakespeare borrows both from Plautus's farce on the mistaken identity of twins (*Menaechmi*) and from Plautus's best-known comedy (*Amphitruo*), in which a husband and his servant are excluded from their own house while a disguised visitor usurps the master's role within. Such ingenious adaptations and rearrangements were common among neoclassical dramatists like Ludovico Ariosto, and, although Shakespeare seems not to have used any of the sixteenth-century analogues to this play, he does reveal an acquaintance with neoclassical comedy and an ability to compete with the best that Europe had to offer in this vein. Such versatility is noteworthy in a young dramatist who was to reveal himself in time as far less of a neoclassicist than a native English writer. Moreover, even if his self-imposed neoclassical training was only an apprenticeship, it was to prove invaluable to Shakespeare. Despite his later tendency toward "romantic" plotting—toward the depiction of multiple actions extending over widely separated spaces and extended periods of time—Shakespeare's greatest comedies continue to point toward the same gratifying resolution of dramatic conflict in a single and well-structured denouement.

For all its Plautine skill of design, *The Comedy of Errors* is quite far removed from *The Menaechmi* in tone and spirit. Gone are the cynicism, the satirical hardness, and the amoral tone of the Roman original. The characters, though still recognizable as types, are humanized. The familiar Plautine parasite is excluded entirely. The usual clever servant happily becomes the Dromio twins. Plautus's quack doctor, Medicus, is hilariously transmuted into Dr. Pinch, a pedantic schoolmaster. The Courtesan's role is no longer prominent. Instead, Shakespeare creates Luciana, the virtuous sister of Adriana, who pleads the cause of forbearance in marriage and who eventually becomes the bride of Antipholus of Syracuse. *The Comedy of Errors* does not end, as do most of Shakespeare's later comedies, with a parade of couples to the altar, but the marriage of Antipholus and Luciana is at least one important step in that direction. Besides, we are told of yet another marriage still to come—that of Dromio of Ephesus to Luce, the kitchen wench. This belowstairs parody of wedded affection is thoroughly English in character and recalls a similar mirroring of courtship among the comic servants of Henry Medwall's *Fulgens and Lucrece* (c. 1497). The motif is not sufficiently stressed to threaten the unity of the main plot, but the potentiality for double plotting is unmistakable.

An even more significant contrast to Plautine farce is to be found in the romantic saga of old Egeon and his long-lost wife, the Abbess. Their story is one not of mistaken identity (though that contributes to the denouement) but of painful separation, wandering, and reunion. Indeed, the note struck at the beginning of the play might seem tragic were we not already attuned to the conventional romantic expectation that separated members of a family are likely to be restored to one another again.

Egeon, threatened with immediate execution, unfolds to us a narrative of wedded bliss interrupted by the malignancy of Fortune. In contrast to the tightly controlled unity of time of the farcical action, the romantic narrative extends (by recollection) over many years of error and suffering. Egeon's tragicomic story of testing and of patient endurance is very much like that of *Apollonius of Tyre*, a popular tale used by Shakespeare in his late romance *Pericles* (c. 1606–1608). The conventions of this sort of romance, ultimately Greek in origin, stress improbability: identical twins who can be told apart only by birthmarks, a storm at sea splitting a vessel in half and neatly dividing a family, and so on. The sea is emblematic of unpredictable Fortune, taking away with one hand and restoring with the other. The wife who is lost at sea, like her counterpart in *Apollonius* or *Pericles*, takes to a life of cloistered devotion, suggesting a pattern of symbolic death, healing, and ultimate rebirth. The ending of *The Comedy of Errors* has just a hint of death restored mysteriously to life: "After so long grief, such nativity!" (5.1.407).

Egeon's story of endurance counterpoints the farce in yet another way. His arraignment before the Duke of Ephesus introduces into the play a "tragic" world of law, punishment, and death. Egeon's date with the executioner is not illusory. His predicament is the result of the bitter "mortal and intestine jars" (1.1.11) between two cities caught in a frenzy of economic reprisals. The law cannot be merciful, even though the unfairness of Egeon's plight is manifest to everyone, including the Duke. These potentially tragic factors must not be overstressed, for the first scene is brief and we are reassured by the play's hilarious tone (and by our surmising that Egeon is father of the Antipholus twins) that all will be well. Still, Shakespeare's addition of this romance plot suggests his restlessness with pure farce. As in his later comedies, which are virtually all threatened by catastrophes, the denouement of *The Comedy of Errors* is deepened into something approaching miraculous recovery. Moreover, the backdrop of a near-tragic world of genuine suffering heightens our appreciation of comic unreality in the self-contained world of Plautine farce and stresses the illusory nature of the dilemmas arising out of purely mistaken identity. Such delusions are all the more comic because they are the delusions that supposedly sane people suffer: contentiousness and jealousy in marriage, concern for respectable appearances among one's neighbors, and the suspicion that one is always being cheated in money matters. These are the chimeras that, by being made to look so plausible and yet so patently insane, are farcically exploited in Shakespeare's comic device: the inversion of madness and sanity, dreaming and waking, illusion and reality.

What happens when the behavior of one twin is mistaken for that of the other? The situation is, of course, amusing in itself, but it also serves as a test of the other characters, to discover what mad hypotheses they will construct. Adriana, faced with her husband's seeming refusal to come home to dinner, launches into a jealous tirade against husbands who neglect their wives for courtesans. The illusory situation, in other words, brings out her latent fears. We understand better now why she acts shrewishly: she fears rejection and the fading of her beauty, and she imagines that her fading beauty may be the cause of her husband's neglect. Actually, even as she speaks, her husband is busy making arrangements about a chain he means to give Adriana; but, when subsequently he is locked out of his own house and jumps to the conclusion that Adriana is being faithless, he resolves in his fury to bestow the chain on a courtesan in order to "spite my wife." He would actually do so were he not saved from this destructively revengeful impulse by the beneficently comic action of the farcical plot: through mistaken identity, the chain is delivered into the hands of his twin. Once again, illusion has prompted a character to assume the worst, to reveal his suspicions of a plot against him. And so it goes when Antipholus of Ephesus is arrested for nonpayment of the chain (he assumes that all merchants are thieves) or is denied his bail money by the servant he thinks he sent to fetch it (he assumes that all servants are thieves). We laugh at the endless capacity of the human mind for distortions of this self-punishing sort.

The metaphor used most often to convey this sense of bewilderment, even a confusion about one's own identity, is that of metamorphosis. All have drunk of Circe's cup (5.1.271) and have been transformed into animals—most of them into asses. All have hearkened to the mermaid's song and are enchanted. Ephesus, they conclude, must be haunted by sorcerers, witches, goblins, and spirits (4.3.11 ff.). Ephesus is, in fact, associated in the Bible with exorcism (Acts 19:13 ff.), and "Circe" suggests that Antipholus of Syracuse is a becalmed Odysseus. In such a mad world, the characters assume a license to embark on Saturnalian holiday. The experience of transformation thus leads to various forms of "release" from ordinary social behavior, but the experience is also disturbing and continually reminds the characters of exorcism, hell, and devils. The threat of incest hovers over the comic business of two brothers sharing a wife, and indeed there is a dark subtext to the twinning that is unavoidably present throughout the play: the twinned cities of Ephesus and Syracuse, the twinned brothers, the twinned servants, all of whom are trying to discover their identities amid the paradoxes of singleness and doubleness. The play's farcical action is never far from violence. Witches and fat kitchen wenches suggest a fascination with unruly women. The characters can explain their inverted world only by assuming that all men are lunatic, all honest women whores, and all true men thieves. "Do you know me, sir? . . . Am I myself?" "Am I in earth, in heaven, or in hell? / Sleeping or waking, mad or well-advised?" (3.2.73–4, 2.2.211–2). Perhaps, as Barbara Freedman suggests, the whole play can be looked at as Egeon's dream. It is both reassuring and hilariously anticlimactic that these questionings can finally be dispelled by the most mundane of explanations: there are two Antipholuses and two Dromios.

Contained within this framework of madness and waking is a playful yet serious examination of the dynamics of courtship and marriage. The two most important women in the play are meaningfully paired and contrasted. Adriana, the shrewish wife, frets at social custom that allows her husband Antipholus to roam abroad while she is domestically confined. Her unmarried sister Luciana endorses the traditional view that husbands enjoy a precedence found everywhere in nature: males "are masters to their females, and their lords" (2.1.24). What Luciana calls obedience (line 29) her married sister calls "servitude" (line 26). Who is right? The debate, left unresolved, nonetheless raises skeptical questions about marital hierarchies. The plot also probes and tests through fantasies of inversion. A wife, believing herself rejected for having aged in her wifely obedience, locks her husband out of the house and dines with a stranger. Luciana meantime finds herself courted by what appears to be her own brother-in-law and thus must face a conflict between desire and loyalty to her sister. Of course, Adriana does not know that she is inverting authority by excluding her husband from his own hearth, but the plot of mistaken identities does allow her to act out her self-assertiveness without being, in fact, guilty of disloyalty. Her husband's role is to play the wandering male and to be eventually forgiven by his wife; presumably his exposure in act 5 will make him a more tolerant husband, like Count Almaviva in Mozart's *The Marriage of Figaro*. The discovery of identities in act 5 allows Luciana to marry the man she has learned to love, but without the guilt of her fantasy experience. Patriarchal values are restored by the play's conclusion, yet the partners in love and marriage have been, to some extent, liberated by their role playing in a plot of metamorphosis. These issues of domestic relations will be further explored in *The Taming of the Shrew*, *Othello*, and other plays.

The playfulness about illusion should not be overemphasized, for the play expends most of its energies in farce. The Dromios, with their incessant drubbings, are often the center of interest in performance, and rightly so. Shakespeare employs no behind-the-scenes manipulator of illusion, such as Puck in *A Midsummer Night's Dream* or the Duke in *Measure for Measure*. His interest in the metaphor of the world as a stage is discernible only as the foreshadowing of greatness to come. Nevertheless, Shakespeare's alterations of Plautus amply reveal the philosophic and idealistic direction that his subsequent comedy is to take.

THE COMEDY OF ERRORS
ON STAGE

    The Comedy of Errors was performed at Gray's Inn, one of the Inns of Court, on December 28, 1594. It appeared at the court of King James I on December 28, 1604. Almost certainly it was acted in public as well, at the Theatre or a similar playhouse. How different were the playing methods called for in these various locales? At Gray's Inn, it has been suggested, Shakespeare's company may have used fixed locations throughout to represent the three houses of Antipholus of Ephesus, the Courtesan, and the Abbess. If so, this is the only time Shakespeare adopted such a staging plan for the entirety of a play. Such uniqueness urges caution in accepting the hypothesis, though it is true that *The Comedy of Errors* is an early play with an unusually direct indebtedness to the classical drama and especially to Plautus's *Menaechmi*. Like its source, *The Comedy of Errors* preserves the unities of place (Ephesus) and time (one day).

    The arguments in favor of fixed locations are as follows. The play requires only an open place, called a "street" or a "mart," as is often the case in classical and neoclassical drama, together with three houses or doors facing onto it. The houses have names, as if they were labeled: Antipholus of Ephesus's house is the Phoenix, the Courtesan's is the Porcupine, and the Abbess's place of residence is the Priory. The use of stage houses with doors was common in performances at court and at the Inns of Court; there, audiences familiar with neoclassical staging would understand the use of a conventionalized facade in arcades, each compartment of which could be used to represent a house. The dialogue and stage directions of Shakespeare's play refer to the three houses as though they are recognizable locations: Antipholus and Dromio of Ephesus enter *"from the Courtesan's"* at 4.1.13, Antipholus and Dromio of Syracuse exit *"to the priory"* at 5.1.37, and a servant exits *"to the Abbess"* at 5.1.282. Dromio of Syracuse's entrance *"from the bay"* (4.1.85) could suggest that one side entrance is understood to lead to the bay, while the other side leads to the town, though with only one such stage direction we cannot be at all sure that the convention was rigorously followed throughout the play.

Against the hypothesis of fixed location is the consideration that Shakespeare's actors would have been hampered in arranging their many exits and entrances not specifically to or from the Phoenix, Porcupine, or Priory. The Priory doorway, not employed until act 5, would have been unavailable to them for most of the action. The play begins with the Duke of Ephesus and others in a location (the Duke's palace? some public place?) that makes no use of the three supposed houses. Quite possibly, even if doorways were marked by placards for a segment of action, the labels could be shifted, letting the middle door for instance represent the Phoenix in act 2, scene 1, and the Porcupine in act 4, scene 1; with rearrangements of this sort, three doorways would suffice. Public theaters such as the Swan, of which a drawing survives, do not seem to have provided the number of doorways called for by neoclassical staging plans. Certainly Shakespeare never limited his acting company this way in any other play.

Moreover, the first scene of act 3 calls for staging effects that seem especially suited to a public theater. Throughout this scene, the theater facade represents the house of Antipholus of Ephesus, into which Antipholus of Syracuse, Adriana, and Luciana have exited at the end of act 2, scene 2, in order to dine "above" (line 206). (The word "above" may or may not refer to a gallery or upper acting area.) Dromio of Syracuse is posted at the door as porter, and need not exit at all as act 2 draws to a close; certainly the sense of location remains continuous as Antipholus of Ephesus and his friends arrive at his door, intending to dine, only to find themselves locked out. Dromio of Syracuse, at the door, may be visible to the audience as he refuses entrance to the irate houseowner and his guests, though they presumably cannot see him. When the maid Luce and then Adriana enter to see what the fuss is about at the door, they probably enter above, in the gallery looking down on the stage, where they can be seen and heard by the audience while presumably invisible to the group at the door. To be sure, this scene must have been staged in some way at Gray's Inn and at court, as well as in the public theater. We are left finally with conflicting indications of mise-en-scène in a play flexibly designed for performance wherever opportunity provided. Still, that very condition of flexibility must have dictated that the play not be staged in too rigorously neoclassical a mode.

However it was originally staged, *The Comedy of Errors* has been the victim ever since of directors who regard it as too inconsequential to survive without adaptation and embellishment. A revival of sorts in 1716, the first recorded since the early seventeenth century, took the form of a farce called *Every Body Mistaken*. The Theatre Royal, Covent Garden, staged in 1734 a comedy in two acts from Plautus and Shakespeare called *See If You Like It; or, 'Tis All a Mistake*. Although something resembling Shakespeare's own *The Comedy of Errors* was performed five times in 1741 at the Theatre Royal, Drury Lane, with Charles Macklin as Dromio of Syracuse, it was in the "improved" versions that the play was generally seen. Thomas Hull was responsible for an adaptation called *The Twins* that was performed again and again at Covent Garden in the late eighteenth century. Hull added songs, intensified the love interest, and elaborated the recognition scene in act 5, trimming the wordplay meanwhile to make room for the improvements. Adriana was provided with a cousin, Hermia, who sang a plaintive song about the love of "forsaken Julia" and her faithless Lysander. W. Woods's *The Twins, or Which Is Which?* (1780, at the Theatre Royal in Edinburgh) reduced the play to a three-act farce lest Shakespeare's "similarity of character, and quick succession of mistakes" should "pall upon an audience." John Philip Kemble retained and further extended the Hull version in 1808 and used this script for many years. All of these adaptations aimed at reducing or concealing the improbability of incident and the occasionally vulgar wit-combat that eighteenth-century taste evidently found indecorous.

Frederic Reynolds carried the idea of musical elaboration to its logical conclusion by turning the play into an opera (Covent Garden, 1819). With lyrics from various Shakespeare plays and sonnets set to the music of Thomas Arne, Mozart, and others, this production sought to repair the deficiencies of a short play. In the process, it restored to the theater a number of songs from *Twelfth Night, As You Like It, Love's Labor's Lost, The Merchant of Venice, Measure for Measure, The Tempest, A Midsummer Night's Dream, Othello,* and *King Lear* that had long been neglected in the performance of those plays. Reynolds added characters with such names as Cerimon and Ctesiphon, and provided a climactic scene of drunkenness in the handsomely furnished house of Balthasar with a spirited rendition of the chorus from *Antony and Cleopatra,* "Come, thou monarch of the vine." The scenery evidently made quite a hit: the last scene of act 3 offered the viewer "a river surrounded by mountains" with snow-covered tops, in front of which Balthasar, Cerimon, and others were seen in hunting costume, crossing a rustic bridge and pausing to sing "When icicles hang by the wall" from *Love's Labor's Lost.*

Samuel Phelps brought back something much closer to Shakespeare's play at the Sadler's Wells Theatre in 1855 and at the Princess's Theatre in 1864, the year of Shakespeare's tercentenary. Phelps's Dromios at the Princess's, the Irish brothers Charles and Harry Webb, with the help of their family resemblance, were able to solve the visual problem of representing identical twins, and the performance without intermission followed all of Shakespeare's scenes in order, though with some cutting. The American actors J. S. Clarke and Harry Paulton were famous as the Dromios in an 1883 production at London's Strand and Opera Comique theaters. In 1895 William Poel with his Elizabethan Stage Society performed the play at Gray's Inn, approximating the conditions of its original staging and delighting George Bernard Shaw: "I am now beginning to cling to

[Poel] as the saviour of theatrical art." Frank Benson played Antipholus of Syracuse in his own production at Stratford-upon-Avon and at London's Coronet Theatre in 1905.

Since then the play has enjoyed a number of successful productions, usually swift-paced and aiming at hilarity, as in the joyous slapstick of Andrew Leigh's version at the Old Vic in 1927, and in Theodore Komisarjevsky's fantastic farce at Stratford-upon-Avon in 1938 with the Antipholus brothers dressed as toreadors in plumed Napoleonic hats and with officers outfitted in tunics and pink bowlers. At the Old Vic, on April 23, 1957, Walter Hudd produced a double bill of *Titus Andronicus* and *The Comedy of Errors* in cut versions edited by John Barton. Both plays were performed in sixteenth-century costume and were presented as the offerings of Elizabethan traveling players at a country inn. In 1962 Clifford Williams's production at Stratford-upon-Avon was energetically played in the manner of the *commedia dell'arte*, while Jean Gascon's 1963 production at Stratford, Ontario, was, as one reviewer called it, a "Punchinello pantomime affair," with five Punchinellos enthusiastically directing the action on stage. *The Boys from Syracuse*, a musical-comedy version of 1938 (subsequently filmed), still draws large audiences when it is revived (as at Stratford, Ontario, in 1986); even today, the hoary device of musically updating, popularizing, and vulgarizing Shakespeare's play seems irresistible. *A New Comedy of Errors, or Too Many Twins* (1940), another musical adaptation put together out of parts of Plautus, Shakespeare, and Molière, was staged in modern dress at London's Mercury Theatre.

The play has been done as Victorian musical comedy (Arts Theatre, Cambridge, England, 1951), as Brechtian folk opera (Arts Theatre, London, 1956), and as a two-ring circus (Delacorte Theater, New York, 1967). It has been set in the American West at the end of the nineteenth century (Stratford, Ontario, 1975); in a provincial Italian town in the 1930s, with the Duke "a broad-bellied Mafioso in a white suit," as the *New York Post* noted (New York, Delacorte Theater, 1975); and in a modern Greek seaside resort (Stratford-upon-Avon, 1976). It has been propped up with a carnival midway complete with ferris wheel and roller coaster (Ashland, Oregon, 1976) and with circus acts such as tumblers and tightrope walkers, as in Robert Woodruff's production at the Goodman Theater in Chicago in 1983 (and brilliantly revived in 1987 at New York's Vivian Beaumont Theater) designed around the Flying Karamazov Brothers' spectacular juggling. The Adriana of this last production, Sophie Hayden, an expert baton twirler, ended her speeches on duty in marriage by spinning her baton far above her head and then casually catching it behind her back.

In 1989, in Stratford, Ontario, Richard Monette directed the play as what he termed "an eighteenth-century rococo divertissement," with ornate carvings and pillars to suggest the sophistication of Ephesus and an energetic, athletic acting style that hurried the story along. Special effects both heightened the strangeness of life in Ephesus and prepared the audience for the wondrous reunion: Luciana, for example, seated on a balcony, released a glittering mechanical butterfly that circled the stage and then slowly climbed into the darkness. The following year in Stratford-upon-Avon, Ian Judge directed the play on an imaginatively simple set, with a Magritte-like blue sky with fluffy white clouds, and a series of doors, either black or white on one side and some vivid color on the other, permitting the play's various slapstick actions. What most distinctly marked this production, however, was that the confusions of identity did not depend upon actors made to look alike, since Des Barrit played both Antipholuses and Graham Turner both Dromios (a device reproduced in 1999 at London's Globe Theatre, with Vicenzo Nicoli playing both Antipholuses and Marcello Magni both Dromios). At the end, of course, additional actors had to be used to speak lines with their backs to the audience, and what actual satisfaction the play offers as identities are sorted and confirmed was thus somewhat weakened by the focus on the theatrical manipulation.

The Brazilian director Caca Rosset mounted a colorful, busy, and noisy *Comedy of Errors* in Central Park as part of the New York Shakespeare Festival in 1992 (with Marisa Tomei as

Adriana). Pennywhistles, buzzers, noisemakers accompanied the slapstick and pratfalls that too often substituted for acting. (One reviewer commented that although this production was sometimes very funny, "I am not sure it would be any less funny if it were being acted in Esperanto or Turkish.") However energetic and theatrically ingenious, there was nothing here of the unnerving quality of a world where identity is so unstable and uncertain. A far more serious version of the play was put on by the RSC at the Other Place in Stratford-upon-Avon in 1996. Tim Supple had the play open in a jail cell with a manacled Egeon attached by a chain to the wall. A bored, impassive Duke added to the danger of the scene. Even when the atmosphere thawed, the comedy found itself in character rather than in mere confusion. Sarah Cameron's Adriana was a woman of obvious sexual appetite, eager to get her husband back in bed (and Robert Bowman's Syracusan Antipholus seemed happily, if exhaustedly, entertained by her confusion); Luciana (Thusita Jayasundera) was an eloquent defender of family values; the two Dromios (Dan Milne and Eric Mallett) were tough, wise-cracking servants, who, had the social order been reversed, would have happily given the beatings they received. The two Antipholuses, wonderfully identical in appearance, were strikingly different in character: the Syracusan, an innocent who almost reluctantly gives in to his good fortune; the Ephesian, angry and controlling. The production was evidence that trusting the text rather than, as so many productions do, submerging it in slapstick results in both good comedy and intelligent theater, as in a different way did Lynne Parker's 2000 production in Stratford-upon-Avon also for the RSC. Here Parker built the production around a series of cinematic references, beginning with the famous image of Harold Lloyd hanging from a clock face and a set that seemed out of *Casablanca*. This production did not eschew farce—indeed the Syracusans (David Tennant as Antipholus; Ian Hughes as Dromio) were a kind of vaudeville team—but the play found a poignancy beneath its slapstick, as again and again characters would enter, just missing a scene that might have clarified their plight, leaving them isolated in their confusion.

Perhaps the many transformations of *The Comedy of Errors* on stage attest to the play's own interest in transformation. Still, it is good to learn from occasional "straight" performances that the script works marvelously when Shakespeare's inventive humor is allowed to speak for itself.

THE COMEDY OF ERRORS
ON SCREEN

Shakespeare could not, of course, have imagined a world in which people would see performances of his plays projected onto large or small screens rather than acted live in theaters, but that has become the case. In the more than one hundred years since the first film of a Shakespeare play was made (in 1899, an excerpt from Sir Herbert Beerbohm Tree's production of *King John*), the screen has become Shakespeare's proper medium no less than the stage or the printed page. If Shakespeare's works are undisputedly literary classics and staples of our theatrical repertories, they have also inescapably become a part of the modern age's love affair with film. In a movie theater, on a television screen, or on a DVD player, Shakespeare's plays live for us, and thereby reach audiences much greater than those that fill our theaters.

It is, however, a development not always welcomed. Some critics complain that Shakespeare on screen is different from (and worse than) Shakespeare in the theater. Certainly it is a distinct experience to see a play in a darkened movie theater with actors larger than life. It is different, too, to see it on a television screen with actors smaller than they are in life, and where the experience of play watching is inevitably more private than in any theater.

But there are obvious advantages as well. On screen, performances are preserved and allowed easily to circulate. If films of Shakespeare may sometimes lack the exhilarating provisionality of live theater, they gain the not insignificant benefit of easy accessibility. In a town without a theater company one can see a Shakespeare play virtually at will. Some newly filmed version of a Shakespeare play is seemingly released every year. A video or DVD can be rented even if the film itself has passed from the local cineplex. And on video we can replay—even interrupt— the performance, allowing it to repeat itself as we attend to details that might otherwise be missed.

Filmed Shakespeare is indeed different from staged Shakespeare or Shakespeare read, but it is no less valuable for being so. It provides a way—and for most of us the most convenient way—to see the plays. For people who cannot get to the theater and who find the printed text difficult to imagine as a theatrical experience, filmed Shakespeare offers easy access to a performance. For students for whom the language of a play often seems (and indeed is) stilted and archaic, the enactment clarifies the psychological and social relations of the characters. For all of us who love Shakespeare, his availability on film gives us an archive of performances to be viewed and enjoyed again and again. It is no less an authentic experience than seeing Shakespeare in the theater, for the modern theater (even the self-conscious anachronisms like the rebuilt Globe) imposes its own anachronisms upon the plays (as indeed does a modern printed edition like this one). And arguably, as many like to claim, if Shakespeare lived today he would most likely have left Stratford for Hollywood.

The Comedy of Errors has not appealed widely to filmmakers, perhaps because it is an early and lesser-known play, perhaps because its trickery of identical twins being mistaken for each other is a theatrical artifice that can work beautifully on stage but may not be well suited to the illusionistic techniques of cinema. Three early silent films, in 1908, 1912, and 1915, did little more than borrow the title for brief bedroom farces. Trevor Nunn's 1976 stage production for the Royal Shakespeare Company was filmed by British commercial television in 1978, providing us with a visual record (available in Great Britain on videocassette) of an essentially theatrical performance. The result is, paradoxically, both a musical comedy and an unsettling exploration of the dark interior that Nunn has uncovered beneath the farcical exterior of the play. The Duke is a fascist tyrant. The Antipholus twins (Mike Gwilym, Roger Rees) and their twin servants, the Dromios (Michael Williams, Nickolas Grace), seem caught in an existential nightmare of mistaken identities, responding like automatons to bewildering and inexplicable confrontations. The women too are anguished: Judi Dench and Francesca Annis are particularly good as Adriana and her sister Luciana, exchanging sororal confidences about what it is like to cope with a man's world in which husbands are prone to dally with flagrant hussies like the Courtesan (Barbara Shelley). The jarring conflict of carnivalesque riot and lighthearted romp makes for a probing film, darkly illuminating.

The BBC series "The Shakespeare Plays" included *The Comedy of Errors* in its sixth season, 1983–4, directed by James Cellan Jones. Pop singer Roger Daltrey doubles as the Dromio twins, while Michael Kitchen doubles as the two Antipholuses, making use of an illusionist trick that sometimes is employed on stage as well (as in the Globe Theatre's production of 1998), albeit with considerable difficulty, since the twins come face-to-face with each other; on film, the matter is technically easy, and perhaps too easy to be satisfying as a viewing experience. Cyril Cusack is eloquently pathetic as old Egeon, father of the Antipholus twins; the part, though limited to the first and last scenes, can be a captivating one, as in Nunn's film with Griffith Jones as a hopelessly addlebrained old codger. Cusack's lengthy recitation of his family's misfortunes in act 1, scene 1 is accompanied by the miming of a troupe dressed in *commedia dell'arte* costuming, whirling their capes to suggest storm winds as they dance on a huge map of the eastern Mediterranean. Duke Solinus (Charles Gray) enters the marketplace in imperial splendor on a white horse, wearing a silver helmet and grotesquely carved silver mask. The chief setting for the play is the handsomely colonnaded marketplace of a Renaissance seaport, along with richly furnished interiors for the domestic scenes inside Antipholus of Ephesus's house. Suzanne Bertish is an articulate Adriana; Wendy Hiller is a formidable Abbess in the final scene.

A videotaped version of 1987 was in effect another televised recording of a stage production, in this case a zany slapstick affair originating at Chicago's Goodman Theatre in 1983–4 and then revived in New York's Vivian Beaumont Theater, with the Flying Karamazov Brothers' circus act aided by the Kamikaze Ground Crew. The circus routines, entertaining enough in their own right, take over the event and overwhelm the spoken language. Adriana (Sophia Hayden in the stage production) twirls a baton as she delivers to Luciana her wifely complaints about a woman's hard lot in marriage; toward the end of her speech, the baton spins up into the air only to be caught behind the actress's back as she finishes her pert oration. Tightrope walkers and trapeze artists defy gravity. The dramatist, Shakespeare, puts in an occasional appearance in glum despair at what is being done to his text, but the implication throughout is that the text itself is so arch and flimsy that it needs heavy doses of vaudeville shtick to render it palatable to today's audiences. The doubling is at times metatheatrically self-aware, as when the abbess Emilia and the Courtesan are played by the same actress (Ethyl Eichelberger). Audiences of both stage production and videotape have professed themselves amused at the result, but some critics have asked the obvious question: if one wants circus, why not go to the circus?

The Boys from Syracuse, a popular musical adaptation by George Abbott with music by Richard Rodgers and Lorenz Hart, was made into a film in 1940. The result is pure camp, rollicking enough for any who are not made uneasy by the freewheeling departures from the original.

The Comedy of Errors
Filmography

1. 1940—*The Boys from Syracuse*
   Universal Pictures
   Jules Levey, producer
   A. Edward Sutherland, director

   Antipholus of Ephesus/Syracuse—Allan Jones
   Dromio of Ephesus/Syracuse—Joe Penner

2. 1954
   BBC
   Lionel Harris, producer
   Lionel Harris, director

> Antipholus of Ephesus—David Pool
> Antipholus of Syracuse—Paul Hansard
> Dromio of Ephesus/Syracuse—James Cairncross
> Adriana—Joan Plowright

3. 1964
   BBC/Royal Shakespeare Company
   Peter Luke and Clifford Williams, producers
   Peter Duguid, director

> Antipholus of Ephesus—Ian Richardson
> Antipholus of Syracuse—Alec McCowen
> Dromio of Ephesus—Clifford Rose
> Dromio of Syracuse—Barry MacGregor
> Adriana—Diana Rigg
> Luciana—Janet Suzman

4. 1978
   Royal Shakespeare Company/ATV
   Cecil Clarke and Peter Roden, producers
   Trevor Nunn and Philip Casson, directors

> Antipholus of Ephesus—Mike Gwilym
> Antipholus of Syracuse—Roger Rees
> Dromio of Ephesus—Nickolas Grace
> Dromio of Syracuse—Michael Williams
> Adriana—Judi Dench
> Luciana—Francesca Annis
> Courtesan—Barbara Shelley
> Egeon—Griffith Jones

5. 1978—*Komediya Oshibok*
   Fridrikh Gorenshtein, director

   > Antipholus of Ephesus/Syracuse—Mikhail
   >   Kozakov
   > Dromio of Ephesus/Syracuse—Mikhail Kononov

6. 1984
   BBC/Time-Life Television
   Shaun Sutton, producer
   James Cellan Jones, director

   > Antipholus of Ephesus/Syracuse—Michael
   >   Kitchen
   > Dromio of Ephesus/Syracuse—Roger Daltrey
   > Adriana—Suzanne Bertish
   > Emilia—Wendy Hiller
   > Egeon—Cyril Cusack
   > Solinus—Charles Gray

7. 1986—*The Boys from Syracuse*
   CBC
   Douglas Campbell, director

   > Antipholus of Ephesus—Colm Feore
   > Antipholus of Syracuse—Geraint Wyn Davies
   > Dromio of Ephesus—Keith Thomas
   > Dromio of Syracuse—Benedict Campbell

8. 1987
   Lincoln Center/PBS
   Bernard Gersten, producer
   Gregory Mosher and Robert Woodruff, directors

   > Antipholus of Ephesus—Howard Jay Patterson
   > Antipholus of Syracuse—Paul Magid
   > Dromio of Ephesus—Randy Nelson

Dromio of Syracuse—Sam Williams
Adriana—Sophie Hayden
Emilia/Courtesan—Ethyl Eichelberger
The Flying Karamazov Brothers

9. 1989 CBC
   Richard Monette, director

   Antipholus of Ephesus/Syracuse—Geordie
     Johnson
   Dromio of Ephesus/Syracuse—Keith Dinicol
   Adriana—Goldie Semple
   Emilia—Wenna Shaw
   Egeon—Nicholas Pennell

10. 2000
    Bob Schulenberg, producer
    Wendell Sweda, director

    Dromio of Syracuse—Garen Michaels
    Adriana—Erika Schikel
    Luciana—Anne von Herrmann
    Egeon—Joseph R. Sicari

This early copy of a drawing by Johannes de Witt of the Swan Theatre in London (c. 1596), made by his friend Arend van Buchell, is the only surviving contemporary sketch of the interior of a public theater in the 1590s.

THE PLAYHOUSE

From other contemporary evidence, including the stage directions and dialogue of Elizabethan plays, we can surmise that the various public theaters where Shakespeare's plays were produced (the Theatre, the Curtain, the Globe) resembled the Swan in many important particulars, though there must have been some variations as well. The public playhouses were essentially round, or polygonal, and open to the sky, forming an acting arena approximately 70 feet in diameter; they did not have a large curtain with which to open and close a scene, such as we see today in opera and some traditional theater. A platform measuring approximately 43 feet across and 27 feet deep, referred to in the de Witt drawing as the *proscaenium*, projected into the yard, *planities sive arena*. The roof, *tectum*, above the stage and supported by two pillars, could contain machinery for ascents and descents, as were required in several of Shakespeare's late plays. Above this roof was a hut, shown in the drawing with a flag flying atop it and a trumpeter at its door announcing the performance of a play. The underside of the stage roof, called the heavens, was usually richly decorated with symbolic figures of the sun, the moon, and the constellations. The platform stage stood at a height of 5½ feet or so above the yard, providing room under the stage for underworldly effects. A trapdoor, which is not visible in this drawing, gave access to the space below.

The structure at the back of the platform (labeled *mimorum aedes*), known as the tiring-house because it was the actors' attiring (dressing) space, featured at least two doors, as shown here. Some theaters seem to have also had a discovery space, or curtained recessed alcove, perhaps between the two doors—in which Falstaff could have hidden from the sheriff (*1 Henry IV*, 2.4) or Polonius could have eavesdropped on Hamlet and his mother (*Hamlet*, 3.4). This discovery space probably gave the actors a means of access to and from the tiring-house. Curtains may also have been hung in front of the stage doors on occasion. The de Witt drawing shows a gallery above the doors that extends across the back and evidently contains spectators. On occasions when action "above" demanded the use of this space, as when Juliet appears at her "window" (*Romeo and Juliet*, 2.2 and 3.5), the gallery seems to have been used by the actors, but large scenes there were impractical.

The three-tiered auditorium is perhaps best described by Thomas Platter, a visitor to London in 1599 who saw on that occasion Shakespeare's *Julius Caesar* performed at the Globe:

> The playhouses are so constructed that they play on a raised platform, so that everyone has a good view. There are different galleries and places [*orchestra, sedilia, porticus*], however, where the seating is better and more comfortable and therefore more expensive. For whoever cares to stand below only pays one English penny, but if he wishes to sit, he enters by another door [*ingressus*] and pays another penny, while if he desires to sit in the most comfortable seats, which are cushioned, where he not only sees everything well but can also be seen, then he pays yet another English penny at another door. And during the performance food and drink are carried round the audience, so that for what one cares to pay one may also have refreshment.

Scenery was not used, though the theater building itself was handsome enough to invoke a feeling of order and hierarchy that lent itself to the splendor and pageantry on stage. Portable properties, such as thrones, stools, tables, and beds, could be carried or thrust on as needed. In the scene pictured here by de Witt, a lady on a bench, attended perhaps by her waiting-gentlewoman, receives the address of a male figure. If Shakespeare had written *Twelfth Night* by 1596 for performance at the Swan, we could imagine Malvolio appearing like this as he bows before the Countess Olivia and her gentlewoman, Maria.

THE COMEDY
OF ERRORS

LUCE, *Adriana's kitchen maid (also known as* NELL)

BALTHASAR, *a merchant*

ANGELO, *a goldsmith*

FIRST MERCHANT, *friend to Antipholus of Syracuse*

SECOND MERCHANT, *to whom Angelo is a debtor*

DOCTOR PINCH, *a conjuring schoolmaster*

A COURTESAN

AN OFFICER

A MESSENGER

Jailer, Headsman, Officers, and other Attendants

SCENE: *Ephesus]*

❧

1.1 *Location: Some editors argue that the play was staged according to classical practice with three visible doors backstage representing three "houses"—that of Antipholus of Ephesus (in the center), that of the Courtesan, and that of the Priory—with the stage itself representing a marketplace or open area. More probably, the stage may have been open and unlocalized. The present scene may be at the Duke's court.*

2 **doom** judgment

3 **Syracusa** Syracuse, in Sicily

4 **partial** predisposed, biased

6 **outrage** violence

8 **wanting guilders** lacking money; the guilder was a Dutch coin worth about one shilling eight pence. **redeem** ransom

9 **sealed** ratified. **bloods** i.e., lives. (The grim analogy is to red sealing wax.)

11 **mortal . . . jars** deadly civil quarrels

13 **synods** assemblies

15 **To . . . towns** to allow no trade between our hostile towns.

16 **Ephesus** a port on the Aegean coast of modern Turkey

17 **marts** markets

20 **confiscate** confiscated. **dispose** disposal

21 **marks** money worth thirteen shillings four pence

22 **quit** pay

23 **Thy substance** The sum total of your wealth

1.1 ✒ *Enter the Duke of Ephesus, with [Egeon] the merchant of Syracuse, Jailer, and other attendants.*

EGEON
Proceed, Solinus, to procure my fall,
And by the doom of death end woes and all.   2

DUKE
Merchant of Syracusa, plead no more.   3
I am not partial to infringe our laws.   4
The enmity and discord which of late
Sprung from the rancorous outrage of your Duke   6
To merchants, our well-dealing countrymen,
Who, wanting guilders to redeem their lives,   8
Have sealed his rigorous statutes with their bloods,   9
Excludes all pity from our threat'ning looks.
For since the mortal and intestine jars   11
Twixt thy seditious countrymen and us,
It hath in solemn synods been decreed,   13
Both by the Syracusians and ourselves,
To admit no traffic to our adverse towns.   15
Nay, more, if any born at Ephesus   16
Be seen at any Syracusian marts and fairs;   17
Again, if any Syracusian born
Come to the bay of Ephesus, he dies,
His goods confiscate to the Duke's dispose,   20
Unless a thousand marks be levièd   21
To quit the penalty and to ransom him.   22
Thy substance, valued at the highest rate,   23
Cannot amount unto a hundred marks;
Therefore by law thou art condemned to die.

32 **unspeakable** indescribable. (But with a punning oxymoron on the literal sense: Egeon will speak that which
cannot be spoken.)

34 **by nature** i.e., by natural affection; here, a father's love

35 **gives me leave** allows me.

37–8 **happy . . . bad** happy except for my misfortune, and
happy indeed through me if we had not suffered misfortune.

41 **Epidamnum** (So spelled in Plautus's *The Menaechmi*);
Epidamnus, a port on the coast of modern Albania.
factor's agent's

42 **care of** anxiety about

52 **As that** they

54 **mean** of low birth

EGEON

    Yet this my comfort: when your words are done,
    My woes end likewise with the evening sun.

DUKE

    Well, Syracusian, say in brief the cause
    Why thou departed'st from thy native home
    And for what cause thou cam'st to Ephesus.

EGEON

    A heavier task could not have been imposed
    Than I to speak my griefs unspeakable.   32
    Yet, that the world may witness that my end
    Was wrought by nature, not by vile offense,   34
    I'll utter what my sorrow gives me leave.   35
    In Syracusa was I born, and wed
    Unto a woman, happy but for me,   37
    And by me, had not our hap been bad.   38
    With her I lived in joy; our wealth increased
    By prosperous voyages I often made
    To Epidamnum, till my factor's death   41
    And the great care of goods at random left   42
    Drew me from kind embracements of my spouse;
    From whom my absence was not six months old
    Before herself, almost at fainting under
    The pleasing punishment that women bear,
    Had made provision for her following me,
    And soon and safe arrivèd where I was.
    There had she not been long but she became
    A joyful mother of two goodly sons,
    And, which was strange, the one so like the other
    As could not be distinguished but by names.   52
    That very hour and in the selfsame inn
    A mean woman was deliverèd   54
    Of such a burden male, twins both alike.
    Those, for their parents were exceeding poor,
    I bought and brought up to attend my sons.

58 **not meanly** to no small degree

59 **motions** proposals, entreaties

62 **league** a measure of distance, about three miles

64 **instance** proof, sign

68 **doubtful** dreadful

72 **plainings** wailings

73 **for fashion** in imitation

74 **delays** i.e., delays from death

77 **sinking-ripe** ready to sink

78 **careful** anxious.   **latter-born** (Compare line 124, however, from which we learn that the younger or "latter-born" was saved with the father.)

84 **whom** those on whom, or, him on whom

86 **straight** at once

89 **vapors** clouds

92 **making amain** proceeding at full speed

93 **Epidaurus** a Greek town southwest of Athens and Corinth; or possibly Dubrovnik, on the Adriatic coast

My wife, not meanly proud of two such boys,   58
Made daily motions for our home return;   59
Unwilling I agreed. Alas, too soon
We came aboard.
A league from Epidamnum had we sailed   62
Before the always-wind-obeying deep
Gave any tragic instance of our harm.   64
But longer did we not retain much hope;
For what obscurèd light the heavens did grant
Did but convey unto our fearful minds
A doubtful warrant of immediate death,   68
Which, though myself would gladly have embraced,
Yet the incessant weepings of my wife—
Weeping before for what she saw must come—
And piteous plainings of the pretty babes,   72
That mourned for fashion, ignorant what to fear,   73
Forced me to seek delays for them and me.   74
And this it was, for other means was none:
The sailors sought for safety by our boat
And left the ship, then sinking-ripe, to us.   77
My wife, more careful for the latter-born,   78
Had fastened him unto a small spare mast
Such as seafaring men provide for storms;
To him one of the other twins was bound,
Whilst I had been like heedful of the other.
The children thus disposed, my wife and I,
Fixing our eyes on whom our care was fixed,   84
Fastened ourselves at either end the mast,
And, floating straight, obedient to the stream,   86
Was carried towards Corinth, as we thought.
At length the sun, gazing upon the earth,
Dispersed those vapors that offended us,   89
And by the benefit of his wishèd light
The seas waxed calm, and we discoverèd
Two ships from far, making amain to us,   92
Of Corinth that, of Epidaurus this.   93

95 **that** that which
98 **had . . . so** i.e., had the gods shown pity
99 **Worthily** justly
103 **helpful ship** i.e., the mast
106 **What** something
107 **as** as if
114 **healthful** saving
115 **reft** bereft
116 **bark** sailing vessel
122 **dilate at full** relate at length

But ere they came—Oh, let me say no more!
Gather the sequel by that went before.   95

DUKE
Nay, forward, old man. Do not break off so,
For we may pity, though not pardon thee.

EGEON
Oh, had the gods done so, I had not now   98
Worthily termed them merciless to us!   99
For, ere the ships could meet by twice five leagues,
We were encountered by a mighty rock,
Which being so violently borne upon,
Our helpful ship was splitted in the midst,   103
So that in this unjust divorce of us
Fortune had left to both of us alike
What to delight in, what to sorrow for.   106
Her part, poor soul, seeming as burdenèd   107
With lesser weight, but not with lesser woe,
Was carried with more speed before the wind,
And in our sight they three were taken up
By fishermen of Corinth, as we thought.
At length, another ship had seized on us,
And, knowing whom it was their hap to save,
Gave healthful welcome to their shipwrecked guests,   114
And would have reft the fishers of their prey   115
Had not their bark been very slow of sail;   116
And therefore homeward did they bend their course.
Thus have you heard me severed from my bliss,
That by misfortunes was my life prolonged,
To tell sad stories of my own mishaps.

DUKE
And, for the sake of them thou sorrowest for,
Do me the favor to dilate at full   122
What have befall'n of them and thee till now.

EGEON
My youngest boy, and yet my eldest care,

127 **so . . . like** in a similar situation

128 **Reft . . . name** (Evidently Egeon, presuming that the lost son and servant are dead, has given their names to the surviving twin brothers.)

130–1 **Whom . . . loved** i.e., while I labored lovingly to find the lost twin, I ran the risk of losing my younger son, whom I loved no less.

133 **clean** entirely.   **bounds** boundaries, territories

134 **coasting** traveling along the coast

135 **Hopeless** despairing

136 **Or** either

138 **timely** speedy, opportune

139 **travels** "travails," or hardships, as well as travels. **warrant** assure

141 **mishap** (Punning on *Hapless* in line 140.)

143 **dignity** high office

144 **would they** even if they wished.   **disannul** annul, cancel

146 **the death** i.e., death by judicial sentence

147 **recalled** revoked

148 **But** except

150 **limit** allow, appoint

At eighteen years became inquisitive
After his brother, and importuned me
That his attendant—so his case was like,   127
Reft of his brother, but retained his name—   128
Might bear him company in the quest of him,
Whom whilst I labored of a love to see,   130
I hazarded the loss of whom I loved.   131
Five summers have I spent in farthest Greece,
Roaming clean through the bounds of Asia,   133
And, coasting homeward, came to Ephesus—   134
Hopeless to find, yet loath to leave unsought   135
Or that or any place that harbors men.   136
But here must end the story of my life,
And happy were I in my timely death   138
Could all my travels warrant me they live.   139

DUKE
Hapless Egeon, whom the fates have marked
To bear the extremity of dire mishap!   141
Now, trust me, were it not against our laws,
Against my crown, my oath, my dignity,   143
Which princes, would they, may not disannul,   144
My soul should sue as advocate for thee.
But though thou art adjudgèd to the death,   146
And passèd sentence may not be recalled   147
But to our honor's great disparagement,   148
Yet will I favor thee in what I can.
Therefore, merchant, I'll limit thee this day   150
To seek thy health by beneficial help.
Try all the friends thou hast in Ephesus;
Beg thou, or borrow, to make up the sum,
And live; if no, then thou art doomed to die.—
Jailer, take him to thy custody.

JAILER
I will, my lord.

158 **procrastinate** postpone

1.2 *Location: The street.*

1 **give out** say

8 **keep** safeguard.

9 **Centaur** the name of an inn, identified by its sign over the door. In mythology, a centaur is half horse, half man.   **host** lodge

11 **dinnertime** i.e., noon.

18 **mean** (1) opportunity (2) money.

19 **villain** servant. (Said good-humoredly.)

21 **humor** mood, disposition

EGEON

    Hopeless and helpless doth Egeon wend,
    But to procrastinate his lifeless end.   *Exeunt.* 158

[1.2]   *Enter Antipholus [of Syracuse], [First] Merchant,
      and Dromio [of Syracuse].*

FIRST MERCHANT

    Therefore give out you are of Epidamnum,   1
    Lest that your goods too soon be confiscate.
    This very day a Syracusian merchant
    Is apprehended for arrival here
    And, not being able to buy out his life,
    According to the statute of the town
    Dies ere the weary sun set in the west.
    There is your money that I had to keep.   8

                    [He gives money.]

S. ANTIPHOLUS *[giving the money to S. Dromio]*

    Go bear it to the Centaur, where we host,   9
    And stay there, Dromio, till I come to thee.
    Within this hour it will be dinnertime.   11
    Till that, I'll view the manners of the town,
    Peruse the traders, gaze upon the buildings,
    And then return and sleep within mine inn,
    For with long travel I am stiff and weary.
    Get thee away.

S. DROMIO

    Many a man would take you at your word
    And go indeed, having so good a mean.   18

                Exit Dromio [of Syracuse].

S. ANTIPHOLUS

    A trusty villain, sir, that very oft,   19
    When I am dull with care and melancholy,
    Lightens my humor with his merry jests.   21

26 **Soon at** About

28 **consort** accompany

30 **lose myself** roam freely

35 **to** in relation to

37 **to . . . forth** to find his companion

38 **confounds himself** mingles indistinguishably.

41 **the almanac . . . date** (Being born in the same hour, Dromio serves as an almanac by which Antipholus can see his age.)

42 **How chance** How comes it

46 **My . . . cheek** i.e., your wife slapped my cheek. (Dromio puns on the idea of the clock *striking* the hour.)

47 **hot** angry

49 **stomach** appetite

What, will you walk with me about the town
And then go to my inn and dine with me?

FIRST MERCHANT
I am invited, sir, to certain merchants,
Of whom I hope to make much benefit;
I crave your pardon. Soon at five o'clock,   26
Please you, I'll meet with you upon the mart
And afterward consort you till bedtime.   28
My present business calls me from you now.

S. ANTIPHOLUS
Farewell till then. I will go lose myself   30
And wander up and down to view the city.

FIRST MERCHANT
Sir, I commend you to your own content.   *Exit.*

S. ANTIPHOLUS
He that commends me to mine own content
Commends me to the thing I cannot get.
I to the world am like a drop of water   35
That in the ocean seeks another drop,
Who, falling there to find his fellow forth,   37
Unseen, inquisitive, confounds himself.   38
So I, to find a mother and a brother,
In quest of them, unhappy, lose myself.

          Enter Dromio of Ephesus.

Here comes the almanac of my true date.—   41
What now? How chance thou art returned so soon?   42

E. DROMIO
Returned so soon? Rather approached too late:
The capon burns, the pig falls from the spit,
The clock hath strucken twelve upon the bell;
My mistress made it one upon my cheek.   46
She is so hot because the meat is cold;   47
The meat is cold because you come not home;
You come not home because you have no stomach;   49

52 **penitent** doing penance (i.e., suffering hunger).
 default fault

53 **wind** i.e., words

56 **crupper** leather strap on a saddle that is passed under
 the horse's tail in order to keep the saddle from riding
 forward.

61 **charge** responsibility

63 **post** haste

64 **post** door-post of a tavern used for keeping reckonings

65 **scour** beat. (With a pun on the idea of keeping score.)

66 **maw** stomach. (Applied usually to animals.)

73 **disposed** disposed of

You have no stomach, having broke your fast.
But we that know what 'tis to fast and pray
Are penitent for your default today.   52

S. ANTIPHOLUS
Stop in your wind, sir. Tell me this, I pray: 53
Where have you left the money that I gave you?

E. DROMIO
Oh—sixpence that I had o'Wednesday last
To pay the saddler for my mistress' crupper?   56
The saddler had it, sir; I kept it not.

S. ANTIPHOLUS
I am not in a sportive humor now.
Tell me, and dally not: where is the money?
We being strangers here, how dar'st thou trust
So great a charge from thine own custody?   61

E. DROMIO
I pray you, jest, sir, as you sit at dinner.
I from my mistress come to you in post;   63
If I return, I shall be post indeed,   64
For she will scour your fault upon my pate.   65
Methinks your maw, like mine, should be your clock   66
And strike you home without a messenger.

S. ANTIPHOLUS
Come, Dromio, come, these jests are out of season;
Reserve them till a merrier hour than this.
Where is the gold I gave in charge to thee?

E. DROMIO
To me, sir? Why, you gave no gold to me.

S. ANTIPHOLUS
Come on, sir knave, have done your foolishness,
And tell me how thou hast disposed thy charge.   73

E. DROMIO
My charge was but to fetch you from the mart

75 **the Phoenix** the sign of Antipholus of Ephesus's shop. (He lives and carries on his business in the same dwelling.) In mythology, a phoenix is a fabulous bird that periodically is regenerated from its own ashes.

79 **sconce** head

80 **stands on** insists on, engages in

90 **hie** hasten

94 **an** if.   **take my heels** take to my heels.

96 **The . . . money** the rascal has cheated me out of all my money.

97 **cozenage** cheating

Home to your house, the Phoenix, sir, to dinner;   75
My mistress and her sister stays for you.

S. ANTIPHOLUS
Now, as I am a Christian, answer me
In what safe place you have bestowed my money,
Or I shall break that merry sconce of yours   79
That stands on tricks when I am undisposed.   80
Where is the thousand marks thou hadst of me?

E. DROMIO
I have some marks of yours upon my pate,
Some of my mistress' marks upon my shoulders,
But not a thousand marks between you both.
If I should pay Your Worship those again,
Perchance you will not bear them patiently.

S. ANTIPHOLUS
Thy mistress' marks? What mistress, slave, hast thou?

E. DROMIO
Your Worship's wife, my mistress at the Phoenix,
She that doth fast till you come home to dinner
And prays that you will hie you home to dinner.   90

S. ANTIPHOLUS
What, wilt thou flout me thus unto my face,
Being forbid? There, take you that, sir knave.

[*He beats Dromio of Ephesus.*]

E. DROMIO
What mean you, sir? For God sake, hold your hands!
Nay, an you will not, sir, I'll take my heels.   94

Exit Dromio of Ephesus.

S. ANTIPHOLUS
Upon my life, by some device or other
The villain is o'erraught of all my money.   96
They say this town is full of cozenage,   97
As nimble jugglers that deceive the eye,
Dark-working sorcerers that change the mind,

101 **mountebanks** charlatans

102 **liberties of sin** persons allowed improper freedom to
    sin. (With a suggestion of certain districts, as in the
    London area, that were exempt from civic jurisdiction
    and were, in a punning sense, places of "license.")

2.1 *Location: The house of Antipholus of Ephesus.*

  8 **Time** Time alone.   **see time** see fit

 11 **still** constantly

 12 **Look when** Whenever

 15 **Why . . . woe** Headstrong liberty (in a wife) is whipped
    and punished with unhappiness. (Luciana argues that a
    wife is better off obeying her husband.)

Soul-killing witches that deform the body,
Disguisèd cheaters, prating mountebanks,   101
And many suchlike liberties of sin.   102
If it prove so, I will be gone the sooner.
I'll to the Centaur to go seek this slave.
I greatly fear my money is not safe.   *Exit.*

2.1 ᴑᴐ *Enter Adriana, wife to Antipholus [of Ephesus],*
       with Luciana, her sister.

ADRIANA
  Neither my husband nor the slave returned
  That in such haste I sent to seek his master?
  Sure, Luciana, it is two o'clock.

LUCIANA
  Perhaps some merchant hath invited him,
  And from the mart he's somewhere gone to dinner.
  Good sister, let us dine, and never fret.
  A man is master of his liberty;
  Time is their master, and when they see time   8
  They'll go or come. If so, be patient, sister.

ADRIANA
  Why should their liberty than ours be more?

LUCIANA
  Because their business still lies out o'door.   11

• ADRIANA
  Look when I serve him so, he takes it ill.   12

LUCIANA
  Oh, know he is the bridle of your will.

ADRIANA
  There's none but asses will be bridled so.

LUCIANA
  Why, headstrong liberty is lashed with woe.   15
  There's nothing situate under heaven's eye

17 **his** its

22 **intellectual sense** reason

25 **accords** consent.

30 **start . . . where** i.e., goes off elsewhere, after other women.

33 **other cause** cause to be otherwise.

34 **A wretched soul** i.e., A fussy, crying baby

39 **helpless** passive

40–1 **But . . . left** i.e., but if you live to see your rights similarly taken away, you will abandon this foolishly urged patience.

But hath his bound, in earth, in sea, in sky.   17
The beasts, the fishes, and the wingèd fowls
Are their males' subjects and at their controls.
Man, more divine, the master of all these,
Lord of the wide world and wild wat'ry seas,
Endued with intellectual sense and souls,   22
Of more preeminence than fish and fowls,
Are masters to their females, and their lords.
Then let your will attend on their accords.   25

ADRIANA
This servitude makes you to keep unwed.

LUCIANA
Not this, but troubles of the marriage bed.

ADRIANA
But, were you wedded, you would bear some sway.

LUCIANA
Ere I learn love, I'll practice to obey.

ADRIANA
How if your husband start some other where?   30

LUCIANA
Till he come home again, I would forbear.

ADRIANA
Patience unmoved! No marvel though she pause;
They can be meek that have no other cause.   33
A wretched soul, bruised with adversity,   34
We bid be quiet when we hear it cry;
But were we burdened with like weight of pain,
As much or more we should ourselves complain.
So thou, that hast no unkind mate to grieve thee,
With urging helpless patience would relieve me;   39
But if thou live to see like right bereft,   40
This fool-begged patience in thee will be left.   41

42 **but to try** i.e., just to put it to the test.

43 **man** servant

45 **at two hands** (Alluding to the beating he received at
1.2.92.)

48 **told** (Punning on "tolled.")

49 **Beshrew** Bad luck to.   **understand** (With pun on
"stand up under"; also in line 53.)

50 **doubtfully** ambiguously

52 **doubtfully** dreadfully

56 **horn-mad** mad as a horned beast. (With a quibble on
the sense of rage at being made a cuckold.)

LUCIANA

Well, I will marry one day, but to try.   42
Here comes your man; now is your husband nigh.   43

Enter Dromio of Ephesus.

ADRIANA

Say, is your tardy master now at hand?

E. DROMIO   Nay, he's at two hands with me, and that   45
my two ears can witness.

ADRIANA

Say, didst thou speak with him? Know'st thou his
mind?

E. DROMIO

I? Ay, he told his mind upon mine ear.   48
Beshrew his hand, I scarce could understand it.   49

LUCIANA

Spake he so doubtfully thou couldst not feel his
meaning?   50

E. DROMIO   Nay, he struck so plainly I could too well
feel his blows, and withal so doubtfully that I could   52
scarce understand them.

ADRIANA

But say, I prithee, is he coming home?
It seems he hath great care to please his wife.

E. DROMIO

Why, mistress, sure my master is horn-mad.   56

ADRIANA

Horn-mad, thou villain?

E. DROMIO   I mean not cuckold-mad,
But sure he is stark mad.
When I desired him to come home to dinner,
He asked me for a thousand marks in gold.
" 'Tis dinnertime," quoth I. "My gold!" quoth he.
"Your meat doth burn," quoth I. "My gold!" quoth he.

66 **Hang up** i.e., To hell with

71 **due . . . tongue** which I should have delivered by my tongue

72 **I bare . . . shoulders** I took in the form of a beating

78 **he . . . cross** i.e., he will add further devotion in the form of a beating. (There is a pun on "to bless," to wound, from the French *blesser. Cross* is a quibble on *across* in the previous line.)

79 **holy** (Punning on the sense "full of holes.")

81 **round** plainspoken. (With pun on the sense of "spherical.")

85 **loureth** frowns, scowls

"Will you come home?" quoth I. "My gold!" quoth he.
"Where is the thousand marks I gave thee, villain?"
"The pig," quoth I, "is burned." "My gold!" quoth he.
"My mistress, sir—" quoth I. "Hang up thy mistress!   66
I know not thy mistress. Out on thy mistress!"

LUCIANA   Quoth who?

E. DROMIO   Quoth my master.
    "I know," quoth he, "no house, no wife, no mistress."
So that my errand, due unto my tongue,   71
I thank him, I bare home upon my shoulders;   72
For, in conclusion, he did beat me there.

ADRIANA
    Go back again, thou slave, and fetch him home.

E. DROMIO
    Go back again and be new beaten home?
    For God's sake, send some other messenger.

ADRIANA
    Back, slave, or I will break thy pate across.

E. DROMIO
    And he will bless that cross with other beating.   78
    Between you I shall have a holy head.   79

ADRIANA
    Hence, prating peasant! Fetch thy master home.

                            [She beats Dromio.]

E. DROMIO
    Am I so round with you as you with me,   81
    That like a football you do spurn me thus?
    You spurn me hence, and he will spurn me hither.
    If I last in this service, you must case me in leather.

                            [Exit.]

LUCIANA
    Fie, how impatience loureth in your face!   85

86 **His . . . grace** He bestows favors on his darling para-
mours

88 **took** taken

89 **wasted** (1) squandered (2) laid waste to, ruined

90 **discourses** conversations

91–2 **If . . . hard** i.e., If my fluent and sometimes too
shrewish discourse seems peevish to my husband, unkindness on his part simply blunts it even more than
when a sharp instrument is struck against hard marble.

93 **his affections bait** entice his passions.

94 **state** outward estate, condition, i.e., clothes.

96 **ground** cause

97 **defeatures** disfigurements.   **decayèd fair** impaired
or perished beauty

99 **pale** enclosure

100 **from** away from.   **stale** rejected lover who has become a laughingstock. (With a pun on *stale*, tiresomely
lacking in freshness; she is stale to him, he dear [*deer*] to
her.)

102 **Unfeeling . . . dispense** Only an insensitive fool
would condone such wrongs.

104 **lets** hinders

106 **Would . . . detain** Would that he would withhold
only that token of his affection

107 **So . . . bed!** provided he would remain faithful to his
marriage bed!

108–12 **I see . . . shame** (A difficult passage. Adriana com-
ments that a showy jewel, like a gaudily dressed woman
[as in line 93], will lose its beauty in time, whereas a
true wife is like gold, which, if properly handled, remains unsullied; no husband of good reputation should
be ashamed of virtuous use like this in his wife.)

109 **his** its

115 **fond** doting

ADRIANA

His company must do his minions grace,   86
Whilst I at home starve for a merry look.
Hath homely age th'alluring beauty took   88
From my poor cheek? Then he hath wasted it.   89
Are my discourses dull? Barren my wit?   90
If voluble and sharp discourse be marred,   91
Unkindness blunts it more than marble hard.   92
Do their gay vestments his affections bait?   93
That's not my fault; he's master of my state.   94
What ruins are in me that can be found
By him not ruined? Then is he the ground   96
Of my defeatures. My decayèd fair   97
A sunny look of his would soon repair.
But, too unruly deer, he breaks the pale   99
And feeds from home. Poor I am but his stale.   100

LUCIANA

Self-harming jealousy! Fie, beat it hence!

ADRIANA

Unfeeling fools can with such wrongs dispense.   102
I know his eye doth homage otherwhere,
Or else what lets it but he would be here?   104
Sister, you know he promised me a chain.
Would that alone o' love he would detain,   106
So he would keep fair quarter with his bed!   107
I see the jewel best enamelèd   108
Will lose his beauty; yet the gold bides still   109
That others touch, and often touching will   110
Wear gold; and no man that hath a name   111
By falsehood and corruption doth it shame.   112
Since that my beauty cannot please his eye,
I'll weep what's left away, and weeping die.

LUCIANA

How many fond fools serve mad jealousy!   115

                              Exeunt.

2.2 *Location: The street before Antipholus of Ephesus's house.*

4 **computation** estimation, reckoning
8 **strokes** blows

[2.2] ⤳ *Enter Antipholus of Syracuse.*

S. ANTIPHOLUS
  The gold I gave to Dromio is laid up
  Safe at the Centaur, and the heedful slave
  Is wandered forth in care to seek me out
  By computation and mine host's report.   4
  I could not speak with Dromio since at first
  I sent him from the mart. See, here he comes.

        Enter Dromio of Syracuse.

  How now, sir, is your merry humor altered?
  As you love strokes, so jest with me again.   8
  You know no Centaur? You received no gold?
  Your mistress sent to have me home to dinner?
  My house was at the Phoenix? Wast thou mad,
  That thus so madly thou didst answer me?

S. DROMIO
  What answer, sir? When spake I such a word?

S. ANTIPHOLUS
  Even now, even here, not half an hour since.

S. DROMIO
  I did not see you since you sent me hence
  Home to the Centaur with the gold you gave me.

S. ANTIPHOLUS
  Villain, thou didst deny the gold's receipt
  And told'st me of a mistress and a dinner,
  For which I hope thou felt'st I was displeased.

S. DROMIO
  I am glad to see you in this merry vein.
  What means this jest? I pray you, master, tell me.

22 **in the teeth** to my face.

24 **earnest** serious. (With a pun on the financial sense: money paid as an installment to secure a bargain.)

28 **jest upon** trifle with

29 **common** public playground

32 **aspect** look, expression; also, astrological favor or disfavor of a planet

34 **sconce** head. (With pun on the meaning "fort" in line 35 and "helmet" or "protective covering" in line 37; the *battering*, lines 35–6, is both a beating and assault by a battering ram.)

36 **An** If

37–8 **insconce** shelter within a sconce or fortification

38–9 **I shall . . . shoulders** i.e., my head will be beaten into my shoulders.

47 **out of season** inappropriately

S. ANTIPHOLUS

    Yea, dost thou jeer and flout me in the teeth?   22

    Think'st thou I jest? Hold, take thou that, and that.

Beats Dromio.

S. DROMIO

    Hold, sir, for God's sake! Now your jest is earnest.   24

    Upon what bargain do you give it me?

S. ANTIPHOLUS

    Because that I familiarly sometimes

    Do use you for my fool and chat with you,

    Your sauciness will jest upon my love   28

    And make a common of my serious hours.   29

    When the sun shines let foolish gnats make sport,

    But creep in crannies when he hides his beams.

    If you will jest with me, know my aspect   32

    And fashion your demeanor to my looks,

    Or I will beat this method in your sconce.   34

S. DROMIO "Sconce" call you it? So you would leave bat-

    tering, I had rather have it a head. An you use these   36

    blows long, I must get a sconce for my head and in-   37

    sconce it too, or else I shall seek my wit in my shoul-   38

    ders. But I pray, sir, why am I beaten?   39

S. ANTIPHOLUS Dost thou not know?

S. DROMIO Nothing, sir, but that I am beaten.

S. ANTIPHOLUS Shall I tell you why?

S. DROMIO Ay, sir, and wherefore; for they say every

    why hath a wherefore.

S. ANTIPHOLUS "Why," first—for flouting me; and then,

    "wherefore"—for urging it the second time to me.

S. DROMIO

    Was there ever any man thus beaten out of season,   47

    When in the why and the wherefore is neither rhyme

        nor reason?

    Well, sir, I thank you.

51 **Marry** i.e., Truly. (A shortened form of the oath "by the Virgin Mary.")

55 **wants that** lacks that which

56 **In good time** Indeed

57 **Basting** (1) Moistening with butter or drippings during cooking (2) Beating.

61 **choleric** (Hot or dry food was thought to produce or aggravate the choleric irascible humor.)

62 **dry basting** hard beating.

73 **fine and recovery** a legal procedure for converting an entailed estate, one in which the property is limited to specified heirs, into a fee simple, one in which the owner has unqualified ownership.

77 **excrement** outgrowth (of hair).

S. ANTIPHOLUS   Thank me, sir, for what?

S. DROMIO   Marry, sir, for this something that you gave   51
me for nothing.

S. ANTIPHOLUS   I'll make you amends next, to give you
nothing for something. But say, sir, is it dinnertime?

S. DROMIO   No, sir, I think the meat wants that I have.   55

S. ANTIPHOLUS   In good time, sir, what's that?   56

S. DROMIO   Basting.   57

S. ANTIPHOLUS   Well, sir, then 'twill be dry.

S. DROMIO   If it be, sir, I pray you, eat none of it.

S. ANTIPHOLUS   Your reason?

S. DROMIO   Lest it make you choleric and purchase me   61
another dry basting.   62

S. ANTIPHOLUS   Well, sir, learn to jest in good time.
There's a time for all things.

S. DROMIO   I durst have denied that before you were
so choleric.

S. ANTIPHOLUS   By what rule, sir?

S. DROMIO   Marry, sir, by a rule as plain as the plain bald
pate of Father Time himself.

S. ANTIPHOLUS   Let's hear it.

S. DROMIO   There's no time for a man to recover his hair
that grows bald by nature.

S. ANTIPHOLUS   May he not do it by fine and recovery?   73

S. DROMIO   Yes, to pay a fine for a periwig and recover
the lost hair of another man.

S. ANTIPHOLUS   Why is Time such a niggard of hair,
being, as it is, so plentiful an excrement?   77

S. DROMIO   Because it is a blessing that he bestows on
beasts, and what he hath scanted men in hair he hath
given them in wit.

83–4 he . . . hair (A reference to the venereal diseases in which loss of hair was a symptom.)

87 dealer i.e., dealer with women

88 a kind of jollity i.e., sexual pleasure.

91 not sound invalid. (With a pun on "venereally diseased.")

93 falsing deceptive. (Continuing the joke on venereal disease.)

97 tiring dressing the hair

105 Time . . . bald (Time is conventionally personified as an old bald man, with only a forelock of hair; one must seize opportunity by the forelock, i.e., quickly, or the occasion will be lost.)

107 bald i.e., senseless, stupid. (Continuing the joke about baldness.)

108 soft gently, wait a minute.   **wafts** beckons

109 strange estranged, distant

110 aspects glances

S. ANTIPHOLUS Why, but there's many a man hath
more hair than wit.

S. DROMIO Not a man of those but he hath the wit to   83
lose his hair.   84

S. ANTIPHOLUS Why, thou didst conclude hairy men
plain dealers without wit.

S. DROMIO The plainer dealer, the sooner lost. Yet he   87
loseth it in a kind of jollity.   88

S. ANTIPHOLUS For what reason?

S. DROMIO For two, and sound ones too.

S. ANTIPHOLUS Nay, not sound, I pray you.   91

S. DROMIO Sure ones, then.

S. ANTIPHOLUS Nay, not sure, in a thing falsing.   93

S. DROMIO Certain ones, then.

S. ANTIPHOLUS Name them.

S. DROMIO The one, to save the money that he spends in
tiring; the other, that at dinner they should not drop in   97
his porridge.

S. ANTIPHOLUS You would all this time have proved
there is no time for all things.

S. DROMIO Marry, and did, sir; namely, e'en no time to
recover hair lost by nature.

S. ANTIPHOLUS But your reason was not substantial
why there is no time to recover.

S. DROMIO Thus I mend it: Time himself is bald and   105
therefore to the world's end will have bald followers.

S. ANTIPHOLUS I knew 'twould be a bald conclusion.   107
But soft, who wafts us yonder?   108

Enter Adriana [beckoning], and Luciana.

ADRIANA
Ay, ay, Antipholus, look strange and frown.   109
Some other mistress hath thy sweet aspects;   110

119 **then** therefore.   **estrangèd from thyself** (1) behaving unlike yourself (2) estranged from me, your other half.

124 **fall** let fall

125 **breaking gulf** surf-crested sea

128 **and . . . too** without taking me from myself (since we are inseparable and indivisible).

129 **the quick** the most sensitive or vulnerable part

131 **consecrate** consecrated

132 **contaminate** contaminated.

133 **spurn** kick

138–43 **I know . . . contagion** i.e., Go ahead and divorce me, since you have the right to do it; because we are one flesh as husband and wife, when you commit adultery it taints me also with the guilt of having been a strumpet. (Said with bitter irony.)

144 **Keep . . . bed** If you remain faithful to your marriage vows

145 **distained** unstained (by contagion)

I am not Adriana, nor thy wife.
The time was once when thou unurged wouldst vow
That never words were music to thine ear,
That never object pleasing in thine eye,
That never touch well welcome to thy hand,
That never meat sweet-savored in thy taste,
Unless I spake, or looked, or touched, or carved to thee.
How comes it now, my husband, oh, how comes it,
That thou art then estrangèd from thyself?   119
Thyself I call it, being strange to me
That, undividable, incorporate,
Am better than thy dear self's better part.
Ah, do not tear away thyself from me!
For know, my love, as easy mayst thou fall   124
A drop of water in the breaking gulf,   125
And take unmingled thence that drop again
Without addition or diminishing,
As take from me thyself and not me too.   128
How dearly would it touch thee to the quick,   129
Shouldst thou but hear I were licentious
And that this body, consecrate to thee,   131
By ruffian lust should be contaminate!   132
Wouldst thou not spit at me, and spurn at me,   133
And hurl the name of husband in my face,
And tear the stained skin off my harlot brow,
And from my false hand cut the wedding ring,
And break it with a deep-divorcing vow?
I know thou canst, and therefore see thou do it.   138
I am possessed with an adulterate blot;   139
My blood is mingled with the crime of lust.   140
For if we two be one, and thou play false,   141
I do digest the poison of thy flesh,   142
Being strumpeted by thy contagion.   143
Keep then fair league and truce with thy true bed,   144
I live distained, thou undishonorèd.   145

149–50 **Who . . . understand** i.e., and I, though listening intently to every word, cannot understand one word of what you've said.

152 **use** treat

160 **compact** plot.

167 **gravity** social dignity

168 **grossly** obviously

169 **Abetting** helping.   **mood** anger.

S. ANTIPHOLUS
    Plead you to me, fair dame? I know you not.
    In Ephesus I am but two hours old,
    As strange unto your town as to your talk,
    Who, every word by all my wit being scanned,   149
    Wants wit in all one word to understand.   150

LUCIANA
    Fie, brother, how the world is changed with you!
    When were you wont to use my sister thus?   152
    She sent for you by Dromio home to dinner.

S. ANTIPHOLUS   By Dromio?

S. DROMIO   By me?

ADRIANA
    By thee; and this thou didst return from him:
    That he did buffet thee and in his blows
    Denied my house for his, me for his wife.

S. ANTIPHOLUS
    Did you converse, sir, with this gentlewoman?
    What is the course and drift of your compact?   160

S. DROMIO
    I, sir? I never saw her till this time.

S. ANTIPHOLUS
    Villain, thou liest, for even her very words
    Didst thou deliver to me on the mart.

S. DROMIO
    I never spake with her in all my life.

S. ANTIPHOLUS
    How can she thus then call us by our names,
    Unless it be by inspiration?

ADRIANA
    How ill agrees it with your gravity   167
    To counterfeit thus grossly with your slave,   168
    Abetting him to thwart me in my mood!   169

170–1 **Be . . . contempt** i.e., It's bad enough that I have to endure your seeing other women; don't make it worse with your contempt.

175 **with . . . communicate** share in your strength.

176 **If . . . dross** If anything usurps my possession of you, it is an impure substance

177 **idle** unprofitable

178 **Who** which.   **want** lack.   **intrusion** forced entry

179 **confusion** ruin.

180 **moves . . . theme** appeals to me as her subject of discourse.

184 **Until . . . uncertainty** Until I can fathom the meaning of what is certainly a mystery. (Stated as an oxymoron.)

185 **entertain** accept.   **fallacy** delusive notion, error.

186 **spread** set the table

187 **beads** rosary beads.

189 **sprites** spirits.

191 **suck our breath** (This piece of folklore was perhaps connected with the old idea that the breath of a person was that person's soul. Fairies were famous for sucking and pinching.)

192 **prat'st thou** do you chatter

193 **sot** fool.

Be it my wrong you are from me exempt,   170
But wrong not that wrong with a more contempt.   171
Come, I will fasten on this sleeve of thine.

[She clings to him.]

Thou art an elm, my husband, I a vine,
Whose weakness, married to thy stronger state,
Makes me with thy strength to communicate.   175
If aught possess thee from me, it is dross,   176
Usurping ivy, brier, or idle moss,   177
Who, all for want of pruning, with intrusion   178
Infect thy sap and live on thy confusion.   179

S. ANTIPHOLUS *[aside]*
To me she speaks; she moves me for her theme.   180
What, was I married to her in my dream?
Or sleep I now and think I hear all this?
What error drives our eyes and ears amiss?
Until I know this sure uncertainty,   184
I'll entertain the offered fallacy.   185

LUCIANA
Dromio, go bid the servants spread for dinner.   186

S. DROMIO
Oh, for my beads! I cross me for a sinner.   187

[He crosses himself.]

This is the fairy land. Oh, spite of spites,
We talk with goblins, elves, and sprites!   189
If we obey them not, this will ensue:
They'll suck our breath or pinch us black and blue.   191

LUCIANA
Why prat'st thou to thyself and answer'st not?   192
Dromio, thou drone, thou snail, thou slug, thou sot!   193

S. DROMIO
I am transformèd, master, am not I?

S. ANTIPHOLUS
I think thou art in mind, and so am I.

197 **ape** i.e., counterfeit.
199 **for grass** for freedom (as a horse put out to pasture).
206 **above** i.e., on the second floor, above Antipholus's shop
207 **shrive** hear confession and give absolution
208 **Sirrah** (Customary form of address to servants.)
209 **forth** away from home
212 **well-advised** in my right mind.
215 **at all adventures** whatever may happen

S. DROMIO
  Nay, master, both in mind and in my shape.

S. ANTIPHOLUS
  Thou hast thine own form.

S. DROMIO   No, I am an ape.   197

LUCIANA
  If thou art changed to aught, 'tis to an ass.

S. DROMIO
  'Tis true; she rides me and I long for grass.   199
  'Tis so, I am an ass; else it could never be
  But I should know her as well as she knows me.

ADRIANA
  Come, come, no longer will I be a fool,
  To put the finger in the eye and weep
  Whilst man and master laughs my woes to scorn.
  Come, sir, to dinner.—Dromio, keep the gate.—
  Husband, I'll dine above with you today   206
  And shrive you of a thousand idle pranks.—   207
  Sirrah, if any ask you for your master,   208
  Say he dines forth, and let no creature enter.—   209
  Come, sister.—Dromio, play the porter well.

S. ANTIPHOLUS [*aside*]
  Am I in earth, in heaven, or in hell?
  Sleeping or waking, mad or well-advised?   212
  Known unto these, and to myself disguised?
  I'll say as they say, and persever so,
  And in this mist at all adventures go.   215

S. DROMIO
  Master, shall I be porter at the gate?

ADRIANA
  Ay, and let none enter, lest I break your pate.

3.1 *Location: Before the house of Antipholus of Ephesus.
The scene is continuous with the previous one.*

2 **keep not hours** am not punctual.

4 **carcanet** necklace (the *chain* of 2.1.105 and line 115
below)

6 **face me down** maintain to my face that

8 **charged him with** entrusted him with possession of

9 **deny** disown

12 **hand** i.e., handiwork on my body. (With a pun on "handwriting.")

17 **at that pass** in that situation

LUCIANA

   Come, come, Antipholus, we dine too late.

         [*Exeunt. Dromio of Syracuse remains as porter,*
         visible to the audience but not to those approaching
         the door.]

3.1 ✑ *Enter Antipholus of Ephesus, his man Dromio,*
     Angelo the goldsmith, and Balthasar the merchant.

E. ANTIPHOLUS

   Good Signor Angelo, you must excuse us all;

   My wife is shrewish when I keep not hours.   2

   Say that I lingered with you at your shop

   To see the making of her carcanet   4

   And that tomorrow you will bring it home.—

   But here's a villain that would face me down   6

   He met me on the mart, and that I beat him

   And charged him with a thousand marks in gold,   8

   And that I did deny my wife and house.—   9

   Thou drunkard, thou, what didst thou mean by this?

E. DROMIO

   Say what you will, sir, but I know what I know.

   That you beat me at the mart, I have your hand to show.   12

   If the skin were parchment and the blows you gave
      were ink,

   Your own handwriting would tell you what I think.

E. ANTIPHOLUS

   I think thou art an ass.

E. DROMIO   Marry, so it doth appear

   By the wrongs I suffer and the blows I bear.

   I should kick, being kicked, and, being at that pass,   17

   You would keep from my heels and beware of an ass.

19 **sad** serious.   **cheer** entertainment

20 **answer** agree with, match

21 **dainties** delicacies.   **cheap** of minor importance.
dear of primary importance.

23 **makes scarce** scarcely equals

24 **every churl** i.e., everyone

27 **sparing** self-denying

28 **cates** provisions, dainties.   **mean** plain, simple

32 **s.d.** *speaking . . . door* (Dromio of Syracuse has remained
on stage since the end of the previous scene, visible to
the audience but not to those at the door. Alternatively,
he could exit at the end of 2.2 and speak now *within*, or
enter at this point, but neither solution seems satisfac-
tory. Compare the entrances of Luce and Adriana at
lines 47 and 60.)

32 **Mome** Dolt, blockhead.   **malt-horse** brewer's horse;
stupid person.   **patch** fool, clown.

33 **hatch** half-door that can be kept closed while the upper
half is opened.

E. ANTIPHOLUS
>You're sad, Signor Balthasar. Pray God our cheer   19
>May answer my good will and your good welcome
>   here.   20

BALTHASAR
>I hold your dainties cheap, sir, and your welcome
>   dear.   21

E. ANTIPHOLUS
>Oh, Signor Balthasar, either at flesh or fish,
>A table full of welcome makes scarce one dainty
>   dish.   23

BALTHASAR
>Good meat, sir, is common; that every churl affords.   24

E. ANTIPHOLUS
>And welcome more common, for that's nothing
>   but words.

BALTHASAR
>Small cheer and great welcome makes a merry feast.

E. ANTIPHOLUS
>Ay, to a niggardly host and more sparing guest.   27
>But though my cates be mean, take them in good
>   part;   28
>Better cheer may you have, but not with better heart.
>   [They approach the door of Antipholus of Ephesus's
>   house.]
>But soft! My door is locked. [To Dromio] Go bid them
>   let us in.

E. DROMIO [calling]
>Maud, Bridget, Marian, Cicely, Gillian, Ginn!

S. DROMIO [speaking from the other side of the door]
>Mome, malt-horse, capon, coxcomb, idiot, patch!   32
>Either get thee from the door or sit down at the
>   hatch.   33

34 **conjure for** summon as if by magic.   **store** quantity

36 **What . . . porter?** i.e., What clown is this who is acting
as gatekeeper?   **stays** waits

37 **on 's** in his

39 **an** if.   **wherefore** why.

42 **owe** own.

45 **The one . . . blame** i.e., My name has never benefited
me, my office of servant has got me much blame.

47 **Thou . . . ass** i.e., you would have been glad to change
places with someone else (since I was beaten like a beast
of burden).

47.1 *Enter Luce* [*above*] (Luce here and then Adriana at
line 60 may enter above in such a way that the audience
understands them not to be visible to those who are calling at the door.)

Dost thou conjure for wenches, that thou call'st for
   such store   34
When one is one too many? Go, get thee from the
   door.

E. DROMIO
What patch is made our porter? My master stays in
   the street.   36

S. DROMIO
Let him walk from whence he came, lest he catch cold
   on 's feet.   37

E. ANTIPHOLUS
Who talks within there? Ho, open the door!

S. DROMIO
Right, sir, I'll tell you when, an you'll tell me
   wherefore.   39

E. ANTIPHOLUS
Wherefore? For my dinner. I have not dined today.

S. DROMIO
Nor today here you must not. Come again when
   you may.

E. ANTIPHOLUS
What art thou that keep'st me out from the house I
   owe?   42

S. DROMIO
The porter for this time, sir, and my name is Dromio.

E. DROMIO
O villain! Thou hast stol'n both mine office and my
   name.
The one ne'er got me credit, the other mickle blame. 45
If thou hadst been Dromio today in my place,
Thou wouldst have changed thy face for a name or
   thy name for an ass.   47

*Enter Luce [above, concealed from Antipholus of
Ephesus and his companions].*

48 **coil** noise, disturbance

51 **Have . . . staff?** Let me come at you with a proverb:
   Shall I take up my abode here? (With a phallic joke.)

52 **When . . . tell?** i.e., Never. (Another proverbial expression, used derisively to turn aside a question.)

54 **minion** hussy.   **hope** (A line following with an an-
   swering rhyme may be missing; perhaps it would have
   cleared up the present obscurity of lines 55 and 56.)

57 **baggage** good-for-nothing

LUCE

    What a coil is there, Dromio? Who are those at the
      gate?   48

E. DROMIO

    Let my master in, Luce.

LUCE   Faith, no, he comes too late,

    And so tell your master.

E. DROMIO   Oh, Lord, I must laugh!

    Have at you with a proverb: Shall I set in my staff?   51

LUCE

    Have at you with another: that's—When, can you
      tell?   52

S. DROMIO

    If thy name be called Luce, Luce, thou hast answered
      him well.

E. ANTIPHOLUS [to Luce]

    Do you hear, you minion? You'll let us in, I hope?   54

LUCE

    I thought to have asked you.

S. DROMIO   And you said no.

E. DROMIO

    So, come help. [They beat the door.] Well struck!
      There was blow for blow.

E. ANTIPHOLUS [to Luce]

    Thou baggage, let me in.

LUCE   Can you tell for whose sake?   57

E. DROMIO

    Master, knock the door hard.

LUCE   Let him knock till it ache.

E. ANTIPHOLUS

    You'll cry for this, minion, if I beat the door down.

                                      [He knocks.]

60 **What . . . town?** i.e., Why do we need to put up with this disturbance, when the town provides stocks for punishment?

61 **keeps** keeps up

65 **If . . . sore** i.e., Yourself and this "knave" she mentions are the same person.   **went** i.e., were

66 **fain** gladly

67 **part** depart

68 **They . . . hither** i.e., Both cheer and welcome have been barred at the door, master. Invite them in. (Said ironically, as an impossibility.)

69 **something . . . wind** something strange going on

70 **You . . . thin** i.e., If you were more thinly dressed (like me), master, you'd say it's a cold wind indeed that shuts you out this way. (Dromio takes the proverbial wind of line 69 in a literal sense.)

LUCE
What needs all that, and a pair of stocks in the town?   60

*Enter Adriana [above, concealed, like Luce and
Dromio of Syracuse, from those at the door].*

ADRIANA
Who is that at the door that keeps all this noise?   61

S. DROMIO
By my troth, your town is troubled with unruly boys.

E. ANTIPHOLUS
Are you there, wife? You might have come before.

ADRIANA
Your wife, sir knave? Go get you from the door.
                                   [Exit with Luce.]

E. DROMIO
If you went in pain, master, this "knave" would go
    sore.   65

ANGELO
Here is neither cheer, sir, nor welcome. We would
    fain have either.   66

BALTHASAR
In debating which was best, we shall part with
    neither.   67

E. DROMIO
They stand at the door, master. Bid them welcome
    hither.   68

E. ANTIPHOLUS
There is something in the wind, that we cannot
    get in.   69

E. DROMIO
You would say so, master, if your garments were thin.   70
Your cake is warm within; you stand here in the
    cold.

72 **as a buck** i.e., as a male deer in rutting season.
(Compare *horn-mad*, 2.1.57.)   **bought and sold** i.e.,
betrayed, ill-treated.

75 **break a word** exchange words. (Punning on *break* in
the previous lines.)

76 **behind** i.e., in farting.

77 **thou . . . breaking** you need to be broken by a beating.
hind boor, menial.

79 **s.d.** *Exit* (If Dromio of Syracuse has been visible to the
audience, he probably leaves at this point.)

80 **crow** crowbar. (Introducing a quibble by Dromio of
Ephesus.)

83 **pluck . . . together** pick a bone together, settle accounts.

87 **draw . . . suspect** bring under suspicion

It would make a man mad as a buck to be so bought
   and sold.   72

E. ANTIPHOLUS
Go fetch me something. I'll break ope the gate.

S. DROMIO
Break any breaking here, and I'll break your knave's
   pate.

E. DROMIO
A man may break a word with you, sir, and words
   are but wind,   75
Ay, and break it in your face, so he break it not
   behind.   76

S. DROMIO
It seems thou want'st breaking. Out upon thee, hind!   77

E. DROMIO
Here's too much "Out upon thee!" I pray thee, let
   me in.

S. DROMIO
Ay, when fowls have no feathers and fish have no
   fin.   [*Exit.*]   79

E. ANTIPHOLUS
Well, I'll break in. Go borrow me a crow.   80

E. DROMIO
A crow without feather? Master, mean you so?
For a fish without a fin, there's a fowl without a
   feather.—
If a crow help us in, sirrah, we'll pluck a crow
   together.   83

E. ANTIPHOLUS
Go, get thee gone. Fetch me an iron crow.

BALTHASAR
Have patience, sir. Oh, let it not be so!
Herein you war against your reputation
And draw within the compass of suspect   87

89 **Once this** To be brief, in short

90 **virtue** merit, general excellence

92 **excuse** justify

93 **made** fastened

95 **the Tiger** (Presumably an inn.)

98 **offer** attempt

99 **stirring passage** bustle

100 **vulgar** public

101 **And . . . rout** and it will be presumed true by everyone

102 **yet . . . estimation** still unsullied reputation

105 **lives upon succession** passes from generation to generation

108 **in . . . mirth** despite my not feeling mirthful, or, in spite of the mockery

112 **desert** my deserving it

115 **this** this time

116 **Porcupine** (The name of the Courtesan's house.)

Th' unviolated honor of your wife.
Once this: your long experience of her wisdom,   89
Her sober virtue, years, and modesty,   90
Plead on her part some cause to you unknown;
And doubt not, sir, but she will well excuse   92
Why at this time the doors are made against you.   93
Be ruled by me. Depart in patience,
And let us to the Tiger all to dinner,   95
And about evening come yourself alone
To know the reason of this strange restraint.
If by strong hand you offer to break in   98
Now in the stirring passage of the day,   99
A vulgar comment will be made of it,   100
And that supposèd by the common rout   101
Against your yet ungallèd estimation,   102
That may with foul intrusion enter in
And dwell upon your grave when you are dead;
For slander lives upon succession,   105
Forever housèd where it gets possession.

E. ANTIPHOLUS
You have prevailed. I will depart in quiet,
And, in despite of mirth, mean to be merry.   108
I know a wench of excellent discourse,
Pretty and witty, wild and yet, too, gentle.
There will we dine. This woman that I mean,
My wife—but, I protest, without desert—   112
Hath oftentimes upbraided me withal.
To her will we to dinner. [To Angelo] Get you home
And fetch the chain; by this I know 'tis made.   115
Bring it, I pray you, to the Porcupine,   116
For there's the house. That chain will I bestow—
Be it for nothing but to spite my wife—
Upon mine hostess there. Good sir, make haste.
Since mine own doors refuse to entertain me,
I'll knock elsewhere, to see if they'll disdain me.

3.2 *Location: Antipholus of Ephesus's house or in front of it, certainly so by line 163.*

1 **may** can

2 **office** duty.

3 **love springs** tender shoots of love

8 **Muffle** hide.   **show of blindness** deceptive appearance.

11 **fair** courteously.   **become disloyalty** carry off your infidelity gracefully

12 **harbinger** messenger, forerunner.

14 **carriage** demeanor

16 **simple** simple-minded.   **attaint** stain, dishonor.

17 **truant with** be faithless to

18 **board** table.

19–20 **Shame . . . word** i.e., Shameful behavior, if cleverly managed, can assume a false reputation for humble conduct, whereas sin is made twice as heinous by callous boasting of it.

22 **Being . . . credit** i.e., we who are wholly inclined to believe you

24 **We . . . turn** we in your orbit are governed by your motion (referring to the motion of the heavenly spheres)

ANGELO
　I'll meet you at that place some hour hence.

E. ANTIPHOLUS
　Do so. This jest shall cost me some expense.　　*Exeunt.*

[3.2] ❧ *Enter Luciana with Antipholus of Syracuse.*

LUCIANA
　And may it be that you have quite forgot　　　　1
　　　A husband's office? Shall, Antipholus,　　　2
　Even in the spring of love, thy love springs rot?　3
　　　Shall love, in building, grow so ruinous?
　If you did wed my sister for her wealth,
　　　Then for her wealth's sake use her with more
　　　　kindness;
　Or if you like elsewhere, do it by stealth:
　　　Muffle your false love with some show of
　　　　blindness.　　　　　　　　　　　　　8
　Let not my sister read it in your eye;
　　　Be not thy tongue thy own shame's orator;
　Look sweet, speak fair, become disloyalty;　　　11
　　　Apparel vice like virtue's harbinger.　　　　12
　Bear a fair presence, though your heart be tainted;
　　　Teach sin the carriage of a holy saint;　　　14
　Be secret-false. What need she be acquainted?
　　　What simple thief brags of his own attaint?　16
　'Tis double wrong to truant with your bed　　　17
　　　And let her read it in thy looks at board.　　18
　Shame hath a bastard fame, well managèd;　　　19
　　　Ill deeds is doubled with an evil word.　　　20
　Alas, poor women! Make us but believe,
　　　Being compact of credit, that you love us.　　22
　Though others have the arm, show us the sleeve;
　　　We in your motion turn and you may move us.　24

27 **holy sport** virtuous jesting. (An oxymoron.)   **vain**
   false

29 **else** otherwise

30 **wonder** miracle.   **hit of** hit upon, guess

31–2 **Less . . . divine** i.e., you seem no less wise and grace-
   ful than our divine queen, wonder of the earth. (Seemingly a flattering reference to Queen Elizabeth.)

34 **Lay . . . conceit** explain to my dull understanding

36 **folded** concealed

37–8 **Against . . . field?** Why do you strive against the pure
   yearning of my soul, as if desiring it to seek elsewhere?

44 **decline** incline.

45 **train** entice.   **mermaid** siren. (In classical myth, one
   of a group of nymphs who lured sailors to destruction
   with their sweet singing.)   **note** song

49 **take** use

51 **die** cease to live. (With a pun on "achieve sexual climax.")

52 **Let . . . sink!** i.e., Love is supposed to be light and frivolous, but this experience of mine would be like drown-
   ing in love, dying thus happily.

53 **reason** talk, argue

54 **mated** amazed, confounded. (With quibble on the sense
   of "matched with a wife.")

Then, gentle brother, get you in again.
    Comfort my sister, cheer her, call her wife.
'Tis holy sport to be a little vain   27
    When the sweet breath of flattery conquers strife.

S. ANTIPHOLUS
Sweet mistress—what your name is else, I know not,   29
    Nor by what wonder you do hit of mine—   30
Less in your knowledge and your grace you show not   31
    Than our earth's wonder, more than earth divine.   32
Teach me, dear creature, how to think and speak;
    Lay open to my earthy-gross conceit,   34
Smothered in errors, feeble, shallow, weak,
    The folded meaning of your words' deceit.   36
Against my soul's pure truth why labor you   37
    To make it wander in an unknown field?   38
Are you a god? Would you create me new?
    Transform me then, and to your power I'll yield.
But if that I am I, then well I know
    Your weeping sister is no wife of mine,
Nor to her bed no homage do I owe.
    Far more, far more to you do I decline.   44
Oh, train me not; sweet mermaid, with thy note,   45
    To drown me in thy sister's flood of tears!
Sing, siren, for thyself, and I will dote.
    Spread o'er the silver waves thy golden hairs,
And as a bed I'll take them and there lie,   49
    And in that glorious supposition think
He gains by death that hath such means to die.   51
    Let Love, being light, be drownèd if she sink!   52

LUCIANA
What, are you mad, that you do reason so?   53

S. ANTIPHOLUS
Not mad, but mated—how, I do not know.   54

LUCIANA
It is a fault that springeth from your eye.

56 **by** near.

58 **As . . . night** i.e., If I were to close my eyes or avert my gaze from you, I might as well be in darkness, unable to see at all.

64 **My sole . . . claim** my sole heaven on earth and my claim on heaven hereafter.

66 **Call . . . thee** i.e., You and I are indivisible, as it were, through the bond of spiritual love, and therefore the sister I love is yourself.

70 **good will** approval. (This is perhaps a mere excuse, but it may be a sign she is attracted.)

S. ANTIPHOLUS
For gazing on your beams, fair sun, being by.   56

LUCIANA
Gaze where you should, and that will clear your sight.

S. ANTIPHOLUS
As good to wink, sweet love, as look on night.   58

LUCIANA
Why call you me "love"? Call my sister so.

S. ANTIPHOLUS
Thy sister's sister.

LUCIANA   That's my sister.

S. ANTIPHOLUS   No,
It is thyself, mine own self's better part,
Mine eye's clear eye, my dear heart's dearer heart,
My food, my fortune, and my sweet hope's aim,
My sole earth's heaven, and my heaven's claim.   64

LUCIANA
All this my sister is, or else should be.

S. ANTIPHOLUS
Call thyself sister, sweet, for I am thee.   66
Thee will I love and with thee lead my life;
Thou hast no husband yet, nor I no wife.
Give me thy hand.

LUCIANA   Oh, soft, sir! Hold you still.
I'll fetch my sister, to get her good will.   *Exit.*   70

Enter Dromio [of] Syracuse, [running].

S. ANTIPHOLUS   Why, how now, Dromio, where runn'st
thou so fast?

S. DROMIO   Do you know me, sir? Am I Dromio? Am I
your man? Am I myself?

S. ANTIPHOLUS   Thou art Dromio, thou art my man,
thou art thyself.

77–8 besides myself also myself. (With a pun on the sense of "out of my mind.")

79 besides (A further quibble: "in addition to.")

86 a beast (With a pun on "abased," reflecting Elizabethan pronunciation of beast as "baste.")

91 without unless.   **"sir-reverence"** i.e. save your reverence, an expression used in apology for the remark that follows it.

92 lean poor, meager

96 grease (With a pun on "grace," reflecting Elizabethan pronunciation.)

98–9 a Poland winter i.e., a long, cold winter.

102 Swart Swarthy, dark

103 She sweats a man She sweats so much that a man

103–4 over shoes ankle-deep. (Her sweat makes mud of her face's grime, so deep that a man would be ankle deep in it.)

106 in grain indelible, fast dyed.

109 Nell (The maidservant appearing in 3.1 is named Luce; usually the two are assumed to be one person.)

S. DROMIO I am an ass, I am a woman's man, and be- 77
sides myself. 78

S. ANTIPHOLUS What woman's man? And how besides 79
thyself?

S. DROMIO Marry, sir, besides myself I am due to a
woman: one that claims me, one that haunts me, one
that will have me.

S. ANTIPHOLUS What claim lays she to thee?

S. DROMIO Marry, sir, such claim as you would lay to
your horse; and she would have me as a beast—not 86
that, I being a beast, she would have me, but that she
being a very beastly creature, lays claim to me.

S. ANTIPHOLUS What is she?

S. DROMIO A very reverend body; ay, such a one as a
man may not speak of without he say "sir-reverence." 91
I have but lean luck in the match, and yet is she a 92
wondrous fat marriage.

S. ANTIPHOLUS How dost thou mean, a fat marriage?

S. DROMIO Marry, sir, she's the kitchen wench, and all
grease, and I know not what use to put her to but to 96
make a lamp of her and run from her by her own light.
I warrant her rags and the tallow in them will burn a 98
Poland winter. If she lives till doomsday, she'll burn a 99
week longer than the whole world.

S. ANTIPHOLUS What complexion is she of?

S. DROMIO Swart like my shoe, but her face nothing like 102
so clean kept. For why? She sweats a man may go over 103
shoes in the grime of it. 104

S. ANTIPHOLUS That's a fault that water will mend.

S. DROMIO No, sir, 'tis in grain. Noah's flood could not 106
do it.

S. ANTIPHOLUS What's her name?

S. DROMIO Nell, sir; but her name and three quarters— 109

110 **an ell** forty-five inches. (With a pun on "a Nell.")

120 **barrenness** callused hardness and dryness. (Perhaps with a pun on "barren ness," a barren promontory.)

123 **reverted** in rebellion. (See the Introduction for an explanation of the reference to the French war.)

124 **heir** (With a pun on "hair" and a joke about syphilis as causing baldness.)

126 **chalky cliffs** i.e., her teeth. (In his geographic metaphor, Dromio of Syracuse identifies white teeth with the cliffs of Dover.)

127 **them** i.e., her teeth.

128 **salt rheum** nasal discharge. (Here Dromio jokingly makes a comparison to the English Channel.)

133–6 **Oh . . . nose** (Dromio imagines whole fleets of Spanish galleons taking on ballast at this woman's nose, embellished as it is with pimples and boils that resemble the treasures pillaged by the Spanish in the Americas. A *carbuncle* is both a precious jewel and a pimple. The eruptions on her nose pay homage [*declining their rich aspect*] to the hot breath of Spain, suggesting both her foul breath and the hot importunity of the Spanish.)

138 **so low** (A joke about the female genitalia. The Netherlands were known as the Low Countries.)

139 **diviner** sorceress

140 **assured** affianced

141 **privy** secret, personal

that's an ell and three quarters—will not measure her 110
from hip to hip.

s. ANTIPHOLUS   Then she bears some breadth?

s. DROMIO   No longer from head to foot than from hip
to hip. She is spherical, like a globe. I could find out
countries in her.

s. ANTIPHOLUS   In what part of her body stands Ireland?

s. DROMIO   Marry, sir, in her buttocks. I found it out by
the bogs.

s. ANTIPHOLUS   Where Scotland?

s. DROMIO   I found it by the barrenness, hard in the 120
palm of the hand.

s. ANTIPHOLUS   Where France?

s. DROMIO   In her forehead, armed and reverted, 123
making war against her heir.   124

s. ANTIPHOLUS   Where England?

s. DROMIO   I looked for the chalky cliffs, but I could find 126
no whiteness in them. But I guess it stood in her chin, 127
by the salt rheum that ran between France and it.   128

s. ANTIPHOLUS   Where Spain?

s. DROMIO   Faith, I saw it not, but I felt it hot in her
breath.

s. ANTIPHOLUS   Where America, the Indies?

s. DROMIO   Oh, sir, upon her nose, all o'er embellished 133
with rubies, carbuncles, sapphires, declining their rich 134
aspect to the hot breath of Spain, who sent whole 135
armadas of carracks to be ballast at her nose.   136

s. ANTIPHOLUS   Where stood Belgia, the Netherlands?

s. DROMIO   Oh, sir, I did not look so low. To conclude, 138
this drudge or diviner laid claim to me, called me 139
Dromio, swore I was assured to her, told me what 140
privy marks I had about me—as the mark of my 141

145 **curtal dog** dog with a docked tail. (And hence not used
    in hunting.)   **turn i'the wheel** run in a wheel to
    turn the spit.

146 **hie thee presently** hasten at once.   **post** hasten.
    road harbor, roadstead.

147 **An if** If

149 **bark** ship

152 **pack** depart

159 **Possessed with** having possession of

162 **to** of

166 **ta'en** overtaken, met up with

shoulder, the mole in my neck, the great wart on my
left arm, that I amazed ran from her as a witch.
And, I think, if my breast had not been made of
    faith and my heart of steel,
She had transformed me to a curtal dog and made
    me turn i'the wheel.   145

S. ANTIPHOLUS
Go, hie thee presently; post to the road.   146
An if the wind blow any way from shore,   147
I will not harbor in this town tonight.
If any bark put forth, come to the mart,   149
Where I will walk till thou return to me.
If everyone knows us and we know none,
'Tis time, I think, to trudge, pack, and be gone.   152

S. DROMIO
As from a bear a man would run for life,
So fly I from her that would be my wife.   *Exit.*

S. ANTIPHOLUS
There's none but witches do inhabit here,
And therefore 'tis high time that I were hence.
She that doth call me husband, even my soul
Doth for a wife abhor. But her fair sister,
Possessed with such a gentle sovereign grace,   159
Of such enchanting presence and discourse,
Hath almost made me traitor to myself.
But, lest myself be guilty to self-wrong,   162
I'll stop mine ears against the mermaid's song.

    Enter Angelo with the chain.

ANGELO
Master Antipholus—
S. ANTIPHOLUS   Ay, that's my name.
ANGELO
I know it well, sir. Lo, here's the chain.
I thought to have ta'en you at the Porcupine;   166

169 **What please yourself** Whatever you please
170 **bespoke** requested
179 **vain** foolish
181 **shifts** stratagems, tricks
184 **straight** at once

4.1 *Location: The street.*

1 **Pentecost** the commemoration of the descent of the
Holy Ghost upon the Apostles, celebrated on the seventh
Sunday after Easter

2 **since** since then.   **importuned** harassed with demands,
bothered

The chain unfinished made me stay thus long.

[*He presents the chain.*]

S. ANTIPHOLUS
What is your will that I shall do with this?

ANGELO
What please yourself, sir. I have made it for you. 169

S. ANTIPHOLUS
Made it for me, sir? I bespoke it not. 170

ANGELO
Not once, nor twice, but twenty times you have.
Go home with it and please your wife withal,
And soon at suppertime I'll visit you
And then receive my money for the chain.

S. ANTIPHOLUS
I pray you, sir, receive the money now,
For fear you ne'er see chain nor money more.

ANGELO
You are a merry man, sir. Fare you well. *Exit.*

S. ANTIPHOLUS
What I should think of this, I cannot tell.
But this I think: there's no man is so vain 179
That would refuse so fair an offered chain.
I see a man here needs not live by shifts, 181
When in the streets he meets such golden gifts.
I'll to the mart and there for Dromio stay;
If any ship put out, then straight away. *Exit.* 184

4.1 ✺ *Enter a* [Second] *Merchant,* [Angelo the]
goldsmith, and an Officer.

SECOND MERCHANT [*to Angelo*]
You know since Pentecost the sum is due, 1
And since I have not much importuned you, 2
Nor now I had not, but that I am bound

4 **want guilders** lack money

5 **present satisfaction** immediate payment

6 **attach** arrest, seize

7 **Even just** Precisely

8 **growing** due, accruing

12 **Pleaseth** May it please

16 **a rope's end** a fragment of rope (to be used as a whip).
    bestow employ

19 **soft** i.e., wait a minute.

21 **I . . . rope!** (An obscure line. Dromio may mean that in
    buying a rope as he is bidden, he is purchasing for him-
    self a thousand poundings or beatings a year.)

22 **holp up** helped

23 **promisèd** was promised

25 **Belike** Perhaps

27 **Saving** With respect for

To Persia and want guilders for my voyage.   4
Therefore make present satisfaction,   5
Or I'll attach you by this officer.   6

ANGELO
Even just the sum that I do owe to you   7
Is growing to me by Antipholus,   8
And in the instant that I met with you
He had of me a chain. At five o'clock
I shall receive the money for the same.
Pleaseth you walk with me down to his house,   12
I will discharge my bond and thank you too.

　　　　Enter Antipholus [and] Dromio of Ephesus
　　　　from the Courtesan's.

OFFICER
That labor may you save. See where he comes.

E. ANTIPHOLUS [*to Dromio of Ephesus*]
While I go to the goldsmith's house, go thou
And buy a rope's end; that will I bestow   16
Among my wife and her confederates
For locking me out of my doors by day.
But soft! I see the goldsmith. Get thee gone.   19
Buy thou a rope and bring it home to me.

E. DROMIO
I buy a thousand pound a year! I buy a rope!   21
　　　　　　　　　　　　　　　　Exit Dromio.

E. ANTIPHOLUS [*to Angelo*]
A man is well holp up that trusts to you!   22
I promisèd your presence and the chain,   23
But neither chain nor goldsmith came to me.
Belike you thought our love would last too long   25
If it were chained together; and therefore came not.

ANGELO [*showing a paper*]
Saving your merry humor, here's the note   27
How much your chain weighs to the utmost carat,

29 **chargeful fashion** expensive workmanship
30 **ducats** gold coins (of several European countries)
32 **discharged** paid
34 **present** available
41 **time enough** in time.
47 **too blame** too blameworthy
48 **dalliance** idle delay
50 **chid** chided
53 **importunes** solicits urgently

The fineness of the gold and chargeful fashion,   29
Which doth amount to three odd ducats more   30
Than I stand debted to this gentleman.
I pray you, see him presently discharged,   32
For he is bound to sea and stays but for it.

E. ANTIPHOLUS
I am not furnished with the present money;   34
Besides, I have some business in the town.
Good signor, take the stranger to my house,
And with you take the chain, and bid my wife
Disburse the sum on the receipt thereof.
Perchance I will be there as soon as you.

ANGELO
Then you will bring the chain to her yourself?

E. ANTIPHOLUS
No, bear it with you, lest I come not time enough.   41

ANGELO
Well, sir, I will. Have you the chain about you?

E. ANTIPHOLUS
An if I have not, sir, I hope you have,
Or else you may return without your money.

ANGELO
Nay, come, I pray you, sir; give me the chain.
Both wind and tide stays for this gentleman,
And I, too blame, have held him here too long.   47

E. ANTIPHOLUS
Good Lord! You use this dalliance to excuse   48
Your breach of promise to the Porcupine.
I should have chid you for not bringing it,   50
But, like a shrew, you first begin to brawl.

SECOND MERCHANT [to Angelo]
The hour steals on. I pray you, sir, dispatch.

ANGELO
You hear how he importunes me. The chain!   53

56 **send me . . . token** send me with some object of yours
   authorizing me to receive payment.

57 **run . . . breath** i.e., carry the joke too far.

59 **brook** endure

60 **whe'er** whether.   **answer me** pay, give me satisfaction

68 **how . . . credit** how it affects my reputation for honesty.

69 **at my suit** on my petition.

71 **touches** injures, affects

E. ANTIPHOLUS
Why, give it to my wife and fetch your money.

ANGELO
Come, come, you know I gave it you even now.
Either send the chain or send me by some token.   56

E. ANTIPHOLUS
Fie, now you run this humor out of breath.   57
Come, where's the chain? I pray you, let me see it.

SECOND MERCHANT
My business cannot brook this dalliance.   59
Good sir, say whe'er you'll answer me or no.   60
If not, I'll leave him to the officer.

E. ANTIPHOLUS
I answer you? What should I answer you?

ANGELO
The money that you owe me for the chain.

E. ANTIPHOLUS
I owe you none till I receive the chain.

ANGELO
You know I gave it you half an hour since.

E. ANTIPHOLUS
You gave me none. You wrong me much to say so.

ANGELO
You wrong me more, sir, in denying it.
Consider how it stands upon my credit.   68

SECOND MERCHANT
Well, officer, arrest him at my suit.   69

OFFICER [to Angelo]
I do, and charge you in the Duke's name to obey me.

ANGELO [to Antipholus of Ephesus]
This touches me in reputation.   71
Either consent to pay this sum for me,
Or I attach you by this officer.

78 **apparently** openly.

84.1 *from the bay* i.e., presumably from a side entry which
we understand to represent the direction of the bay.

89 **balsamum** balm, a fragrant and healing resin.   **aqua
vitae** strong liquor.

90 **in her trim** rigged and ready to sail

93 **peevish** silly.   **sheep** (With play on *ship* in next line.)

95 **waftage** passage.

E. ANTIPHOLUS

    Consent to pay thee that I never had?
    Arrest me, foolish fellow, if thou dar'st.

ANGELO

    Here is thy fee. Arrest him, officer. [*He gives money.*]
    I would not spare my brother in this case
    If he should scorn me so apparently.   78

OFFICER [*to Antipholus of Ephesus*]

    I do arrest you, sir. You hear the suit.

E. ANTIPHOLUS

    I do obey thee till I give thee bail.—
    But, sirrah, you shall buy this sport as dear
    As all the metal in your shop will answer.

ANGELO

    Sir, sir, I shall have law in Ephesus,
    To your notorious shame, I doubt it not.   84

      Enter Dromio [of] Syracuse, from the bay.

S. DROMIO

    Master, there's a bark of Epidamnum
    That stays but till her owner comes aboard,
    And then she bears away. Our freightage, sir,
    I have conveyed aboard, and I have bought
    The oil, the balsamum, and aqua vitae.   89
    The ship is in her trim; the merry wind   90
    Blows fair from land; they stay for naught at all
    But for their owner, master, and yourself.

E. ANTIPHOLUS

    How now? A madman? Why, thou peevish sheep,   93
    What ship of Epidamnum stays for me?

S. DROMIO

    A ship you sent me to, to hire waftage.   95

E. ANTIPHOLUS

    Thou drunken slave, I sent thee for a rope
    And told thee to what purpose and what end.

98 **a rope's end** i.e., a whipping, or perhaps a hangman's noose; see line 16 and note

101 **list** listen to

110 **Dowsabel** (Used ironically for Nell or Luce; derived from the French *douce et belle*, "gentle and beautiful.")

111 **compass** achieve. (With added meaning of "put my arms around.")

4.2 *Location: The house of Antipholus of Ephesus.*

2 **austerely** objectively, strictly

4 **or red** either red-faced.   **or sad** either sad

6 **meteors tilting** i.e., passions warring. (The next line begins a passage of stichomythia, dialogue in which each speech consists of a single line, much used in classical drama.)

7 **no** i.e., any

S. DROMIO

You sent me for a rope's end as soon.   98
You sent me to the bay, sir, for a bark.

E. ANTIPHOLUS

I will debate this matter at more leisure
And teach your ears to list me with more heed.   101
To Adriana, villain, hie thee straight. [*He gives a key.*]
Give her this key, and tell her, in the desk
That's covered o'er with Turkish tapestry
There is a purse of ducats; let her send it.
Tell her I am arrested in the street,
And that shall bail me. Hie thee, slave, begone!
On, officer, to prison till it come.

Exeunt [all but Dromio of Syracuse].

S. DROMIO

To Adriana! That is where we dined,
Where Dowsabel did claim me for her husband.   110
She is too big, I hope, for me to compass.   111
Thither I must, although against my will,
For servants must their masters' minds fulfill.   *Exit.*

[4.2] ✧ *Enter Adriana and Luciana.*

ADRIANA

Ah, Luciana, did he tempt thee so?
Mightst thou perceive austerely in his eye   2
That he did plead in earnest, yea or no?
Looked he or red or pale, or sad or merrily?   4
What observation mad'st thou in this case
Of his heart's meteors tilting in his face?   6

LUCIANA

First he denied you had in him no right.   7

8 **spite** vexation, grief.

10 **true . . . were** i.e., though no foreigner, he spoke true in the sense that he is a stranger to my heart and thus false to his vows.

14 **honest** honorable

16 **Didst . . . fair?** Did you encourage him?

18 **his** its

19 **sere** withered

20 **shapeless** misshapen

22 **Stigmatical in making** deformed in appearance

26 **And . . . worse** i.e., and yet I wish that others would look disapprovingly at his behavior, or would find him less attractive.

ADRIANA

He meant he did me none; the more my spite.   8

LUCIANA

Then swore he that he was a stranger here.

ADRIANA

And true he swore, though yet forsworn he were.   10

LUCIANA

Then pleaded I for you.

ADRIANA   And what said he?

LUCIANA

That love I begged for you he begged of me.

ADRIANA

With what persuasion did he tempt thy love?

LUCIANA

With words that in an honest suit might move.   14
First he did praise my beauty, then my speech.

ADRIANA

Didst speak him fair?

LUCIANA   Have patience, I beseech.   16

ADRIANA

I cannot, nor I will not, hold me still.
My tongue, though not my heart, shall have his will.   18
He is deformèd, crooked, old, and sere,   19
Ill faced, worse bodied, shapeless everywhere;   20
Vicious, ungentle, foolish, blunt, unkind,
Stigmatical in making, worse in mind.   22

LUCIANA

Who would be jealous then of such a one?
No evil lost is wailed when it is gone.

ADRIANA

Ah, but I think him better than I say,
And yet would herein others' eyes were worse.   26

27 **Far . . . away** i.e., I am like the lapwing (a bird that flies away from its nest to divert the attention of intruders from its young) in that what I say is very different from what I feel

29 **Sweet** (An inoffensive term of endearment. Some editors emend it to *Sweat*.)

32 **Tartar limbo** Tartarus or pagan hell, worse than Christian hell

33 **everlasting garment** i.e., buff leather attire of the police officer; everlasting both because of its durability and because of the joke about perpetual durance in limbo or jail. (*Everlasting* is itself the name of a coarse woolen fabric sometimes used for the uniforms of petty officers of justice.)

35 **fairy** i.e., malevolent spirit

37–9 **one . . . well** i.e., one who prohibits the movement of people in alleys and narrow passages; a hound that follows a trail in the direction opposite to that which the game has taken (with a quibble on *counter*, a prison) and skillfully tracks game by the mere scent of the footprint

40 **judgment** legal decision. (With a pun on "Judgment Day," continuing the joke about jail as Tartar limbo.)

42 **'rested on the case** arrested in a lawsuit.

45 **suit** (1) suit of clothes (2) lawsuit

Far from her nest the lapwing cries away;   27
  My heart prays for him, though my tongue do curse.

Enter Dromio of Syracuse, [running, with the key].

S. DROMIO
  Here, go—the desk, the purse! Sweet, now, make
    haste.   29

LUCIANA
  How hast thou lost thy breath?

S. DROMIO   By running fast.

ADRIANA
  Where is thy master, Dromio? Is he well?

S. DROMIO
  No, he's in Tartar limbo, worse than hell.   32
  A devil in an everlasting garment hath him,   33
  One whose hard heart is buttoned up with steel;
  A fiend, a fairy, pitiless and rough;   35
  A wolf, nay, worse, a fellow all in buff;
  A back friend, a shoulder clapper, one that
    countermands   37
  The passages of alleys, creeks, and narrow lands;   38
  A hound that runs counter and yet draws dryfoot
    well;   39
  One that before the judgment carries poor souls to
    hell.   40

ADRIANA   Why, man, what is the matter?

S. DROMIO
  I do not know the matter. He is 'rested on the case.   42

ADRIANA
  What, is he arrested? Tell me at whose suit.

S. DROMIO
  I know not at whose suit he is arrested well;
  But is in a suit of buff which 'rested him, that can I
    tell.   45

49 **band** bond. (But Dromio puns on the sense "neckband" in the next line.)

54 **one** (*One* and *on* were pronounced very much alike; the word here rhymes with *gone*.)

56 **if . . . fear** Time appears to go backward, like a person in debt (an "over," punning on *hour*), or a whore (pronounced like *hour*) running away from an arresting officer.   **'a** it, she, he

57 **fondly** foolishly

58 **Time . . . season** i.e., Having overspent itself, Time is so much in debt that it is of little worth when it comes to fruition. (With a probable pun on *season* and *seisin*, legal possession.)   **to season** to bring to fruition, make acceptable.

61 **theft** i.e., a thief.   **in the way** lying in wait to arrest

Will you send him, mistress, redemption, the
    money in his desk?

ADRIANA
    Go fetch it, sister.   *Exit Luciana.*
                    This I wonder at,
    That he, unknown to me, should be in debt.
    Tell me, was he arrested on a band?   49

S. DROMIO
    Not on a band, but on a stronger thing:
    A chain, a chain! Do you not hear it ring?

ADRIANA   What, the chain?

S. DROMIO
    No, no, the bell. 'Tis time that I were gone.
    It was two ere I left him, and now the clock strikes
        one.   54

ADRIANA
    The hours come back! That did I never hear.

S. DROMIO
    Oh, yes, if any hour meet a sergeant, 'a turns back for
        very fear.   56

ADRIANA
    As if Time were in debt. How fondly dost thou
        reason!   57

S. DROMIO
    Time is a very bankrupt and owes more than he's
        worth to season.   58
    Nay, he's a thief too. Have you not heard men say
    That Time comes stealing on by night and day?
    If 'a be in debt and theft, and a sergeant in the way,   61
    Hath he not reason to turn back an hour in a day?

        Enter Luciana [with the purse].

63 **straight** straightaway, immediately

65 **conceit** imaginings

66 **Conceit . . . injury** (Adriana is filled with imaginings, both of the wrongs she has suffered and the comfort she can provide her wayward husband.)

4.3 *Location: The street.*

4 **tender** offer

5 **other** others

10 **imaginary wiles** tricks of the imagination

11 **Lapland sorcerers** (Lapland was said to surpass all nations in the practice of witchcraft and sorcery.)

13–14 **What . . . new-appareled?** (Dromio wonders how his master has managed to evade the arresting officer who apprehended Antipholus [of Ephesus, not Syracuse] in 4.1. *New-appareled* plays on [1] a new suit of clothes [2] a new lawsuit. Adam, *new-appareled* in beasts' skins after the fall of man [Genesis 3:21], reminds Dromio of the correcting officer in his buff leather jerkin or jacket.)

16 **kept the Paradise** (This sounds like an allusion to an inn of which the innkeeper was named Adam.)

18 **calf's . . . Prodigal** (An allusion to the fatted calf killed for the Prodigal Son's return; see Luke 15:23.)

ADRIANA

Go, Dromio, there's the money. Bear it straight,   63
And bring thy master home immediately.

                    [*Exit Dromio, with the purse.*]

Come, sister. I am pressed down with conceit—   65
Conceit, my comfort and my injury.   *Exeunt.*   66

[4.3] ❧ *Enter Antipholus of Syracuse, [wearing the chain].*

S. ANTIPHOLUS

There's not a man I meet but doth salute me
As if I were their well-acquainted friend,
And everyone doth call me by my name.
Some tender money to me; some invite me;   4
Some other give me thanks for kindnesses;   5
Some offer me commodities to buy.
Even now a tailor called me in his shop
And showed me silks that he had bought for me
And therewithal took measure of my body.
Sure, these are but imaginary wiles,   10
And Lapland sorcerers inhabit here.   11

          Enter Dromio of Syracuse, [with the purse].

S. DROMIO Master, here's the gold you sent me for.
What, have you got the picture of old Adam new-   13
appareled?   14

S. ANTIPHOLUS

What gold is this? What Adam dost thou mean?

S. DROMIO Not that Adam that kept the Paradise, but   16
that Adam that keeps the prison; he that goes in the
calf's skin that was killed for the Prodigal; he that   18
came behind you, sir, like an evil angel, and bid you
forsake your liberty.

S. ANTIPHOLUS I understand thee not.

23 **case** (With a pun on *plain case,* line 22.)

24 **a sob** (1) a sob of pity; see next line (2) a breathing-space given to a horse to allow it to recover from its exertions

24–5 **'rests them** (1) arrests them (2) gives them respite

25 **decayed** financially ruined. (With a pun on the usual sense.)

26 **durance** a kind of long-wearing cloth like buff. (With a pun on "imprisonment.")   **sets . . . rest** stakes his all. (With a continuing pun on *'rest;* the metaphor of staking all one's venture is from the game of primero.)

27 **mace** staff of office carried by a constable.   **morris-pike** a weapon, supposedly of Moorish origin

29 **band** troop

30 **band** bond

32 **rest** (Continuing the wordplay on *arrest.*)

37 **hoy** a small coastal vessel

38 **angels** gold coins worth about ten shillings

40 **distract** deranged, distracted

46 **avoid!** begone! (See Matthew 4:10.)

49 **dam** mother

50 **habit** demeanor, manner; also, dress.   **light** wanton

S. DROMIO   No? Why, 'tis a plain case: he that went, like
a bass viol, in a case of leather, the man, sir, that,   23
when gentlemen are tired, gives them a sob and 'rests   24
them; he, sir, that takes pity on decayed men and gives   25
them suits of durance; he that sets up his rest to do   26
more exploits with his mace than a morris-pike.   27

S. ANTIPHOLUS   What, thou mean'st an officer?

S. DROMIO   Ay, sir, the sergeant of the band; he that   29
brings any man to answer it that breaks his band; one   30
that thinks a man always going to bed, and says, "God
give you good rest!"   32

S. ANTIPHOLUS   Well, sir, there rest in your foolery. Is
there any ships puts forth tonight? May we be gone?

S. DROMIO   Why, sir, I brought you word an hour since
that the bark *Expedition* put forth tonight, and then
were you hindered by the sergeant to tarry for the hoy   37
Delay. Here are the angels that you sent for to deliver   38
you.   [*He gives the purse.*]

S. ANTIPHOLUS
The fellow is distract, and so am I,   40
And here we wander in illusions.
Some blessèd power deliver us from hence!

      Enter a Courtesan.

COURTESAN
Well met, well met, Master Antipholus.
I see, sir, you have found the goldsmith now.
Is that the chain you promised me today?

S. ANTIPHOLUS
Satan, avoid! I charge thee, tempt me not.   46

S. DROMIO   Master, is this Mistress Satan?

S. ANTIPHOLUS   It is the devil.

S. DROMIO   Nay, she is worse, she is the devil's dam, and   49
here she comes in the habit of a light wench; and   50

51 **damn me** i.e., dam me, make me a mother.

53 **angels of light** (See 2 Corinthians 11:14, where Satan is referred to as transformed into an angel of light.)

54 **ergo** therefore

55 **will burn** i.e., will transmit venereal disease.

57 **mend** supplement, complete

58 **spoon meat** food for infants, hence delicacies

59 **bespeak** order

61–2 **he . . . devil** (A proverbial idea.)

63 **What** Why

73 **An if** If

77 **Avaunt** Begone

thereof comes that the wenches say, "God damn me,"   51
that's as much to say, "God make me a light wench."
It is written they appear to men like angels of light;   53
light is an effect of fire, and fire will burn; ergo, light   54
wenches will burn. Come not near her.   55

COURTESAN
  Your man and you are marvelous merry, sir.
  Will you go with me? We'll mend our dinner here.   57

S. DROMIO   Master, if you do, expect spoon meat, or   58
bespeak a long spoon.   59

S. ANTIPHOLUS   Why, Dromio?

S. DROMIO   Marry, he must have a long spoon that must   61
eat with the devil.   62

S. ANTIPHOLUS [to the Courtesan]
  Avoid then, fiend! What tell'st thou me of supping?   63
  Thou art, as you are all, a sorceress.
  I conjure thee to leave me and be gone.

COURTESAN
  Give me the ring of mine you had at dinner
  Or, for my diamond, the chain you promised,
  And I'll be gone, sir, and not trouble you.

S. DROMIO
  Some devils ask but the parings of one's nail,
  A rush, a hair, a drop of blood, a pin,
  A nut, a cherrystone;
  But she, more covetous, would have a chain.
  Master, be wise. An if you give it her,   73
  The devil will shake her chain and fright us with it.

COURTESAN
  I pray you, sir, my ring, or else the chain!
  I hope you do not mean to cheat me so?

S. ANTIPHOLUS
  Avaunt, thou witch!—Come, Dromio, let us go.   77

78 **"Fly . . . peacock** (The peacock, symbol of vanity, warns hypocritically against pride; similarly, in Dromio's view, this cheating courtesan accuses Antipholus of cheating her. *Pride* can also mean "sexual desire.")

80 **demean** conduct

85 **rage** madness

88 **Belike** Presumably

90 **My way** My best course

92 **perforce** forcibly

93 **fittest** as most appropriate

4.4 *Location: The street.*

3 **warrant thee** guarantee your security

4 **wayward** perverse, ill tempered

5 **lightly trust** easily believe

6 **attached** arrested

S. DROMIO
"Fly pride," says the peacock. Mistress, that you
    know.   *Exeunt [Antipholus and Dromio of Syracuse].*   78

COURTESAN
Now, out of doubt Antipholus is mad,
Else would he never so demean himself.   80
A ring he hath of mine worth forty ducats,
And for the same he promised me a chain;
Both one and other he denies me now.
The reason that I gather he is mad,
Besides this present instance of his rage,   85
Is a mad tale he told today at dinner
Of his own doors being shut against his entrance.
Belike his wife, acquainted with his fits,   88
On purpose shut the doors against his way.
My way is now to hie home to his house   90
And tell his wife that, being lunatic,
He rushed into my house and took perforce   92
My ring away. This course I fittest choose,   93
For forty ducats is too much to lose.   *[Exit.]*

[4.4] ❧ *Enter Antipholus of Ephesus with a Jailer [or
    Officer].*

E. ANTIPHOLUS
Fear me not, man, I will not break away.
I'll give thee ere I leave thee so much money
To warrant thee as I am 'rested for.   3
My wife is in a wayward mood today   4
And will not lightly trust the messenger.   5
That I should be attached in Ephesus,   6
I tell you, 'twill sound harshly in her ears.

    Enter Dromio of Ephesus with a rope's end.

14 **I'll . . . rate** I'll supply you with five hundred ropes, sir, for that amount.

22 **Good now** Pray you

27 **sensible in** sensitive to; also, made sensible by

30 **ears** (With a pun on "years"; Dromio says he is an ass for having served his master so long.)

Here comes my man. I think he brings the money.—
How now, sir? Have you that I sent you for?

E. DROMIO [*giving the rope*]
Here's that, I warrant you, will pay them all.

E. ANTIPHOLUS   But where's the money?

E. DROMIO
Why, sir, I gave the money for the rope.

E. ANTIPHOLUS
Five hundred ducats, villain, for a rope?

E. DROMIO
I'll serve you, sir, five hundred at the rate.   14

E. ANTIPHOLUS
To what end did I bid thee hie thee home?

E. DROMIO   To a rope's end, sir; and to that end am I
returned.

E. ANTIPHOLUS
And to that end, sir, I will welcome you.

> [*He starts to beat Dromio of Ephesus.*]

OFFICER   Good sir, be patient.

E. DROMIO   Nay, 'tis for me to be patient. I am in adversity.

OFFICER   Good now, hold thy tongue.   22

E. DROMIO   Nay, rather persuade him to hold his hands.

E. ANTIPHOLUS   Thou whoreson, senseless villain!

E. DROMIO   I would I were senseless, sir, that I might not
feel your blows.

E. ANTIPHOLUS   Thou art sensible in nothing but blows,   27
and so is an ass.

E. DROMIO   I am an ass, indeed; you may prove it by my
long ears. I have served him from the hour of my   30
nativity to this instant and have nothing at his hands
for my service but blows. When I am cold, he heats me
with beating; when I am warm, he cools me with

37 **wont** is accustomed to (bear)

41 *respice finem* consider your end. (A pious sentiment on the brevity of life and the approach of death; with a play on *respice funem,* "consider the hangman's rope." A parrot might be taught to say *respice finem,* or perhaps "rope.")

47 **Doctor** (An honorific term for any learned person. Pinch is not a medical doctor.)   **conjurer** (Being able to speak Latin, Pinch could conjure spirits.)

48 **true sense** right mind

49 **please** pay

50 **sharp** angry

51 **ecstasy** fit, frenzy.

beating. I am waked with it when I sleep, raised with
it when I sit, driven out of doors with it when I go
from home, welcomed home with it when I return.
Nay, I bear it on my shoulders, as a beggar wont her   37
brat, and I think when he hath lamed me I shall beg
with it from door to door.

> *Enter Adriana, Luciana, Courtesan, and a school-*
> *master called Pinch.*

E. ANTIPHOLUS
Come, go along. My wife is coming yonder.

E. DROMIO [*to Adriana*]   Mistress, *respice finem*, respect   41
your end; or rather, to prophesy like the parrot,
"Beware the rope's end."

E. ANTIPHOLUS   Wilt thou still talk?   *Beats Dromio.*

COURTESAN [*to Adriana*]
How say you now? Is not your husband mad?

ADRIANA
His incivility confirms no less.——
Good Doctor Pinch, you are a conjurer;   47
Establish him in his true sense again,   48
And I will please you what you will demand.   49

LUCIANA
Alas, how fiery and how sharp he looks!   50

COURTESAN
Mark how he trembles in his ecstasy!   51

PINCH [*to Antipholus*]
Give me your hand, and let me feel your pulse.

E. ANTIPHOLUS [*striking him*]
There is my hand, and let it feel your ear.

PINCH
I charge thee, Satan, housed within this man,
To yield possession to my holy prayers

60 **minion** hussy, i.e., Adriana

61 **companion** fellow, i.e., Pinch.   **saffron** yellow

66 **would** I wish

71 **Pardie** (An oath, from the French *pardieu*, "by God.")

73 **Sans** Without

75 **Certes** Certainly.   **kitchen vestal** (Ironically, her task was like that of the vestal virgins of ancient Rome, to keep the fire burning.)

And to thy state of darkness hie thee straight!
I conjure thee by all the saints in heaven!

E. ANTIPHOLUS
Peace, doting wizard, peace! I am not mad.

ADRIANA
Oh, that thou wert not, poor distressèd soul!

E. ANTIPHOLUS
You minion, you, are these your customers?   60
Did this companion with the saffron face   61
Revel and feast it at my house today,
Whilst upon me the guilty doors were shut
And I denied to enter in my house?

ADRIANA
Oh, husband, God doth know you dined at home,
Where would you had remained until this time,   66
Free from these slanders and this open shame!

E. ANTIPHOLUS
Dined at home? [*To E. Dromio*] Thou villain, what
    sayest thou?

E. DROMIO
Sir, sooth to say, you did not dine at home.

E. ANTIPHOLUS
Were not my doors locked up and I shut out?

E. DROMIO
Pardie, your doors were locked and you shut out.   71

E. ANTIPHOLUS
And did not she herself revile me there?

E. DROMIO
Sans fable, she herself reviled you there.   73

E. ANTIPHOLUS
Did not her kitchen maid rail, taunt, and scorn me?

E. DROMIO
Certes, she did. The kitchen vestal scorned you.   75

79 **soothe** encourage, humor.   **contraries** denials, lies.

80–1 **It . . . frenzy** i.e., Such a humoring of Antipholus is
not reprehensible. Dromio grasps the nature of his master's madness, and giving in this way can soothe the patient's frenzy.

82 **suborned** induced

85 **Heart . . . might** You might have sent love and good
wishes by me

86 **rag** scrap

93 **deadly** deathlike

94 **bound . . . room** (The regular treatment for lunacy in
Shakespeare's day.)

E. ANTIPHOLUS
And did not I in rage depart from thence?

E. DROMIO
In verity you did. My bones bears witness,
That since have felt the vigor of his rage.

ADRIANA
Is't good to soothe him in these contraries?   79

PINCH
It is no shame. The fellow finds his vein,   80
And yielding to him humors well his frenzy.   81

E. ANTIPHOLUS [to Adriana]
Thou hast suborned the goldsmith to arrest me.   82

ADRIANA
Alas, I sent you money to redeem you
By Dromio here, who came in haste for it.

E. DROMIO
Money by me? Heart and good will you might,   85
But surely, master, not a rag of money.   86

E. ANTIPHOLUS
Went'st not thou to her for a purse of ducats?

ADRIANA
He came to me, and I delivered it.

LUCIANA
And I am witness with her that she did.

E. DROMIO
God and the rope maker bear me witness
That I was sent for nothing but a rope!

PINCH [to Adriana]
Mistress, both man and master is possessed;
I know it by their pale and deadly looks.   93
They must be bound and laid in some dark room.   94

95 **forth** out. (Also in line 97.)

102 **pack** i.e., of conspirators

103 **abject scorn** despicable object of contempt

106.1 *offer* attempt

111 **make a rescue** take a prisoner by force from legal custody.   **Masters** Good sirs

E. ANTIPHOLUS [to Adriana]
    Say wherefore didst thou lock me forth today?   95
    [To E. Dromio] And why dost thou deny the bag of gold?

ADRIANA
    I did not, gentle husband, lock thee forth.

E. DROMIO
    And, gentle master, I received no gold.
    But I confess, sir, that we were locked out.

ADRIANA
    Dissembling villain, thou speak'st false in both.

E. ANTIPHOLUS
    Dissembling harlot, thou art false in all
    And art confederate with a damnèd pack   102
    To make a loathsome abject scorn of me!   103
    But with these nails I'll pluck out those false eyes
    That would behold in me this shameful sport.

                              [He threatens Adriana.]

ADRIANA
    Oh, bind him, bind him! Let him not come near me.   106

        Enter three or four, and offer to bind him. He
        strives.

PINCH
    More company! The fiend is strong within him.

LUCIANA
    Ay me, poor man, how pale and wan he looks!

E. ANTIPHOLUS
    What, will you murder me?—Thou jailer, thou,
    I am thy prisoner. Wilt thou suffer them
    To make a rescue?

OFFICER   Masters, let him go.   111
    He is my prisoner, and you shall not have him.

114 **peevish** silly, senseless

116 **displeasure** injury, wrong

119 **discharge** pay, clear the debt for

121 **knowing . . . grows** when I know how the debt accrued

123 **unhappy** fatal, miserable

125 **entered in bond** (1) bound up, tied (2) pledged

126 **mad** exasperate

129 **idly** senselessly

130.2 *Manent* They remain on stage

PINCH
Go bind his man, for he is frantic too.

[They bind Dromio of Ephesus.]

ADRIANA
What wilt thou do, thou peevish officer?   114
Hast thou delight to see a wretched man
Do outrage and displeasure to himself?   116

OFFICER
He is my prisoner. If I let him go,
The debt he owes will be required of me.

ADRIANA
I will discharge thee ere I go from thee.   119
Bear me forthwith unto his creditor,
And, knowing how the debt grows, I will pay it.   121
Good Master Doctor, see him safe conveyed
Home to my house. Oh, most unhappy day!   123

E. ANTIPHOLUS   Oh, most unhappy strumpet!

E. DROMIO
Master, I am here entered in bond for you.   125

E. ANTIPHOLUS
Out on thee, villain! Wherefore dost thou mad me?   126

E. DROMIO   Will you be bound for nothing? Be mad,
good master; cry, "The devil!"

LUCIANA
God help, poor souls, how idly do they talk!   129

ADRIANA
Go bear him hence. Sister, go you with me.   130

> *Exeunt [Pinch and his assistants, carrying off*
> *Antipholus and Dromio of Ephesus]. Manent*
> *Officer, Adriana, Luciana, Courtesan.*

Say now, whose suit is he arrested at?

OFFICER
One Angelo, a goldsmith. Do you know him?

136 **bespeak** order
137 **Whenas** When
143 **at large** in full, in detail.
145 **naked** drawn
146.1 *omnes* all

ADRIANA
I know the man. What is the sum he owes?

OFFICER
Two hundred ducats.

ADRIANA   Say, how grows it due?

OFFICER
Due for a chain your husband had of him.

ADRIANA
He did bespeak a chain for me, but had it not.   136

COURTESAN
Whenas your husband all in rage today   137
Came to my house and took away my ring—
The ring I saw upon his finger now—
Straight after did I meet him with a chain.

ADRIANA
It may be so, but I did never see it.—
Come, jailer, bring me where the goldsmith is.
I long to know the truth hereof at large.   143

> *Enter Antipholus and Dromio [of] Syracuse with*
> *their rapiers drawn.*

LUCIANA
God, for thy mercy! They are loose again.

ADRIANA
And come with naked swords. Let's call more help   145
To have them bound again.

OFFICER   Away! They'll kill us.   146

> *Run all out. Exeunt omnes, as fast as may be,*
> *frighted. [Antipholus and Dromio of Syracuse*
> *remain.]*

S. ANTIPHOLUS
I see these witches are afraid of swords.

S. DROMIO
She that would be your wife now ran from you.

149 **stuff** goods, baggage

152 **speak us fair** speak courteously to us

155 **still** always

5.1 *Location: Before the priory and Antipholus of Ephesus's house.*

1 **hindered you** delayed your journey

8 **might bear** is worth

10 **self** same

S. ANTIPHOLUS
   Come to the Centaur. Fetch our stuff from thence.   149
   I long that we were safe and sound aboard.

S. DROMIO   Faith, stay here this night. They will surely
   do us no harm. You saw they speak us fair, give us   152
   gold. Methinks they are such a gentle nation that, but
   for the mountain of mad flesh that claims marriage of
   me, I could find in my heart to stay here still and turn   155
   witch.

S. ANTIPHOLUS
   I will not stay tonight for all the town.
   Therefore, away, to get our stuff aboard.   *Exeunt.*

5.1 ❧ *Enter the [Second] Merchant and [Angelo] the*
       goldsmith.

ANGELO
   I am sorry, sir, that I have hindered you;   1
   But I protest he had the chain of me,
   Though most dishonestly he doth deny it.

SECOND MERCHANT
   How is the man esteemed here in the city?

ANGELO
   Of very reverend reputation, sir,
   Of credit infinite, highly beloved,
   Second to none that lives here in the city.
   His word might bear my wealth at any time.   8

SECOND MERCHANT
   Speak softly. Yonder, as I think, he walks.

       Enter Antipholus and Dromio [of Syracuse] again,
       [Antipholus wearing the chain].

ANGELO
   'Tis so, and that self chain about his neck   10

11 **forswore** denied under oath

16 **circumstance** details, particulars

18 **charge** cost

19 **honest** honorable

20 **on** as a result of

29 **impeach** accuse

31 **presently** at once.   **stand** take a fighting stance, put yourself to the test.

32 **defy** challenge.   **villain** base person.

Which he forswore most monstrously to have.   11
Good sir, draw near to me. I'll speak to him.—
Signor Antipholus, I wonder much
That you would put me to this shame and trouble
And, not without some scandal to yourself,
With circumstance and oaths so to deny   16
This chain which now you wear so openly.
Beside the charge, the shame, imprisonment,   18
You have done wrong to this my honest friend,   19
Who, but for staying on our controversy,   20
Had hoisted sail and put to sea today.
This chain you had of me. Can you deny it?

S. ANTIPHOLUS
I think I had. I never did deny it.

SECOND MERCHANT
Yes, that you did, sir, and forswore it too.

S. ANTIPHOLUS
Who heard me to deny it or forswear it?

SECOND MERCHANT
These ears of mine, thou know'st, did hear thee.
Fie on thee, wretch! 'Tis pity that thou liv'st
To walk where any honest men resort.

S. ANTIPHOLUS
Thou art a villain to impeach me thus.   29
I'll prove mine honor and mine honesty
Against thee presently, if thou dar'st stand.   31

SECOND MERCHANT
I dare, and do defy thee for a villain.   *They draw.*   32

> Enter Adriana, Luciana, [the] Courtesan, and
> others.

ADRIANA
Hold, hurt him not, for God sake! He is mad.

34 **within him** under his guard
36 **take** take refuge in
37 **spoiled** ruined, done for.
45 **This week** All this week.   **sad** melancholy
48 **brake** broke.   **rage** madness.
49 **wreck of** shipwreck at
51 **Strayed** led astray

Some get within him; take his sword away.   34
Bind Dromio too, and bear them to my house.

S. DROMIO
Run, master, run; for God sake, take a house!   36
This is some priory. In, or we are spoiled!   37

Exeunt [Antipholus and Dromio of Syracuse]
to the priory.

Enter [Emilia, the] Lady Abbess.

ABBESS
Be quiet, people. Wherefore throng you hither?

ADRIANA
To fetch my poor distracted husband hence.
Let us come in, that we may bind him fast
And bear him home for his recovery.

ANGELO
I knew he was not in his perfect wits.

SECOND MERCHANT
I am sorry now that I did draw on him.

ABBESS
How long hath this possession held the man?

ADRIANA
This week he hath been heavy, sour, sad,   45
And much different from the man he was;
But till this afternoon his passion
Ne'er brake into extremity of rage.   48

ABBESS
Hath he not lost much wealth by wreck of sea?   49
Buried some dear friend? Hath not else his eye
Strayed his affection in unlawful love—   51
A sin prevailing much in youthful men,
Who give their eyes the liberty of gazing?
Which of these sorrows is he subject to?

57 **reprehended** rebuked
60 **Haply** Perhaps
62 **copy** topic, theme.   **conference** conversation.
63 **for** because of
66 **glancèd** alluded to
67 **Still** continually
69 **venom** venomous

ADRIANA

To none of these, except it be the last,
Namely, some love that drew him oft from home.

ABBESS

You should for that have reprehended him.   57

ADRIANA

Why, so I did.

ABBESS   Ay, but not rough enough.

ADRIANA

As roughly as my modesty would let me.

ABBESS

Haply in private.

ADRIANA   And in assemblies too.   60

ABBESS   Ay, but not enough.

ADRIANA

It was the copy of our conference.   62
In bed he slept not for my urging it;   63
At board he fed not for my urging it;
Alone, it was the subject of my theme;
In company I often glancèd it;   66
Still did I tell him it was vile and bad.   67

ABBESS

And thereof came it that the man was mad.
The venom clamors of a jealous woman   69
Poisons more deadly than a mad dog's tooth.
It seems his sleeps were hindered by thy railing,
And thereof comes it that his head is light.
Thou say'st his meat was sauced with thy upbraidings.
Unquiet meals make ill digestions;
Thereof the raging fire of fever bred,
And what's a fever but a fit of madness?
Thou sayest his sports were hindered by thy brawls.
Sweet recreation barred, what doth ensue
But moody and dull melancholy,

82 **distemperatures** physical disorder, illness
84 **mad or** madden either
88 **demeaned** behaved, conducted
90 **She . . . reproof** i.e., She led me to see my own faults.
97 **assaying** attempting
99 **office** duty
100 **attorney** agent, deputy
103 **approvèd** proved, tested
105 **formal** normal, made in proper form

Kinsman to grim and comfortless despair,
And at her heels a huge infectious troop
Of pale distemperatures and foes to life?   82
In food, in sport, and life-preserving rest
To be disturbed would mad or man or beast.   84
The consequence is, then, thy jealous fits
Hath scared thy husband from the use of wits.

LUCIANA
  She never reprehended him but mildly,
  When he demeaned himself rough, rude, and wildly.   88
  [*To Adriana*] Why bear you these rebukes and
        answer not?

ADRIANA
  She did betray me to my own reproof.—   90
  Good people, enter and lay hold on him.

ABBESS
  No, not a creature enters in my house.

ADRIANA
  Then let your servants bring my husband forth.

ABBESS
  Neither. He took this place for sanctuary,
  And it shall privilege him from your hands
  Till I have brought him to his wits again
  Or lose my labor in assaying it.   97

ADRIANA
  I will attend my husband, be his nurse,
  Diet his sickness, for it is my office,   99
  And will have no attorney but myself;   100
  And therefore let me have him home with me.

ABBESS
  Be patient, for I will not let him stir
  Till I have used the approvèd means I have,   103
  With wholesome syrups, drugs, and holy prayers,
  To make of him a formal man again.   105

106 **parcel** integral part
118 **By this** By this time.　　**dial** sundial or watch dial
121 **sorry** sad

It is a branch and parcel of mine oath,   106
A charitable duty of my order.
Therefore depart and leave him here with me.

ADRIANA
I will not hence and leave my husband here;
And ill it doth beseem your holiness
To separate the husband and the wife.

ABBESS
Be quiet and depart. Thou shalt not have him. [Exit.]

LUCIANA [to Adriana]
Complain unto the Duke of this indignity.

ADRIANA
Come, go. I will fall prostrate at his feet
And never rise until my tears and prayers
Have won His Grace to come in person hither
And take perforce my husband from the Abbess.

SECOND MERCHANT
By this, I think, the dial points at five.   118
Anon, I'm sure, the Duke himself in person
Comes this way to the melancholy vale,
The place of death and sorry execution   121
Behind the ditches of the abbey here.

ANGELO   Upon what cause?

SECOND MERCHANT
To see a reverend Syracusian merchant,
Who put unluckily into this bay
Against the laws and statutes of this town,
Beheaded publicly for his offense.

ANGELO
See where they come. We will behold his death.

LUCIANA
Kneel to the Duke before he pass the abbey.

132 **so . . . him** so much consideration we grant him. (With suggestion also of "value" and "have pity on.")

138 **important** importunate, pressing.   **letters** (Adriana would seem to have been ward to the Duke and married at his importunate urging.)

140 **That desperately** so that recklessly

141 **all** totally

142 **displeasure** wrong, injury

144 **rage** madness, insanity

146 **take order** settle, make reparation

148 **wot** know.   **strong** violent

152 **bent** turned

Enter the Duke of Ephesus and [Egeon] the
merchant of Syracuse, barehead [and bound], with
the Headsman and other officers.

DUKE

Yet once again proclaim it publicly,
If any friend will pay the sum for him,
He shall not die; so much we tender him.   132

ADRIANA [*kneeling*]

Justice, most sacred Duke, against the Abbess!

DUKE

She is a virtuous and a reverend lady.
It cannot be that she hath done thee wrong.

ADRIANA

May it please Your Grace, Antipholus my husband,
Who I made lord of me and all I had,
At your important letters, this ill day   138
A most outrageous fit of madness took him,
That desperately he hurried through the street—   140
With him his bondman, all as mad as he—   141
Doing displeasure to the citizens   142
By rushing in their houses, bearing thence
Rings, jewels, anything his rage did like.   144
Once did I get him bound and sent him home,
Whilst to take order for the wrongs I went   146
That here and there his fury had committed.
Anon, I wot not by what strong escape,   148
He broke from those that had the guard of him,
And with his mad attendant and himself,
Each one with ireful passion, with drawn swords,
Met us again and, madly bent on us,   152
Chased us away, till raising of more aid
We came again to bind them. Then they fled
Into this abbey, whither we pursued them;
And here the Abbess shuts the gates on us

160 **help** cure.

162 **engaged** pledged

167 **determine** settle

168 **shift** escape, depart

170 **a-row** one after another

173 **puddled** from filthy puddles

175 **nicks . . . fool** gives him a fantastic haircut in the short
fashion of the court fool

183 **scorch** (Compare the singeing of Pinch's beard at line
171; also, score, slash.)

And will not suffer us to fetch him out,
Nor send him forth that we may bear him hence.
Therefore, most gracious Duke, with thy command
Let him be brought forth and borne hence for help.   160

DUKE [*raising Adriana*]
Long since, thy husband served me in my wars,
And I to thee engaged a prince's word,   162
When thou didst make him master of thy bed,
To do him all the grace and good I could.—
Go, some of you, knock at the abbey gate
And bid the Lady Abbess come to me.
I will determine this before I stir.   167

Enter a [Servant as] messenger.

SERVANT
Oh, mistress, mistress, shift and save yourself!   168
My master and his man are both broke loose,
Beaten the maids a-row, and bound the doctor,   170
Whose beard they have singed off with brands of fire,
And ever as it blazed they threw on him
Great pails of puddled mire to quench the hair.   173
My master preaches patience to him, and the while
His man with scissors nicks him like a fool;   175
And sure, unless you send some present help,
Between them they will kill the conjurer.

ADRIANA
Peace, fool! Thy master and his man are here,
And that is false thou dost report to us.

SERVANT
Mistress, upon my life, I tell you true.
I have not breathed almost since I did see it.
He cries for you, and vows, if he can take you,
To scorch your face and to disfigure you.   183

Cry within.

Hark, hark! I hear him, mistress. Fly, begone!

185 **halberds** long-handled spears with blades.

188 **housed him in** i.e., drove him into

192 **bestrid** stood over (to defend when fallen in battle)

199 **abusèd** maltreated

203 **Discover** Reveal

205 **harlots** rascals, vile companions

DUKE

Come, stand by me. Fear nothing.—Guard with
  halberds!   185

ADRIANA

Ay me, it is my husband! Witness you
That he is borne about invisible.
Even now we housed him in the abbey here,   188
And now he's there, past thought of human reason.

Enter Antipholus and Dromio of Ephesus.

E. ANTIPHOLUS

Justice, most gracious Duke, oh, grant me justice!
Even for the service that long since I did thee,
When I bestrid thee in the wars and took   192
Deep scars to save thy life; even for the blood
That then I lost for thee, now grant me justice.

EGEON

Unless the fear of death doth make me dote,
I see my son Antipholus and Dromio.

E. ANTIPHOLUS

Justice, sweet prince, against that woman there!
She whom thou gav'st to me to be my wife,
That hath abusèd and dishonored me   199
Even in the strength and height of injury!
Beyond imagination is the wrong
That she this day hath shameless thrown on me.

DUKE

Discover how, and thou shalt find me just.   203

E. ANTIPHOLUS

This day, great Duke, she shut the doors upon me
While she with harlots feasted in my house.   205

DUKE

A grievous fault. Say, woman, didst thou so?

208 **So . . . soul** i.e., As I hope to be saved

209 **he . . . withal** he charges me with.

210 **on** at

214 **am advisèd** know very well

219 **packed** in conspiracy

221 **parted with** departed from

227 **swear me down** swear in the face of my denials

233 **fairly** civilly.   **bespoke** requested

ADRIANA

No, my good lord. Myself, he, and my sister
Today did dine together. So befall my soul   208
As this is false he burdens me withal.   209

LUCIANA

Ne'er may I look on day nor sleep on night   210
But she tells to Your Highness simple truth.

ANGELO

Oh, perjured woman!—They are both forsworn.
In this the madman justly chargeth them.

E. ANTIPHOLUS

My liege, I am advisèd what I say,   214
Neither disturbèd with the effect of wine
Nor heady-rash provoked with raging ire,
Albeit my wrongs might make one wiser mad.
This woman locked me out this day from dinner.
That goldsmith there, were he not packed with her,   219
Could witness it, for he was with me then;
Who parted with me to go fetch a chain,   221
Promising to bring it to the Porcupine,
Where Balthasar and I did dine together.
Our dinner done, and he not coming thither,
I went to seek him. In the street I met him,
And in his company that gentleman.

                    [*Indicating the Second Merchant.*]
There did this perjured goldsmith swear me down   227
That I this day of him received the chain,
Which, God he knows, I saw not; for the which
He did arrest me with an officer.
I did obey, and sent my peasant home
For certain ducats. He with none returned.
Then fairly I bespoke the officer   233
To go in person with me to my house.
By th' way we met
My wife, her sister, and a rabble more

239 **mere anatomy** absolute skeleton.   **mountebank**
    quack, charlatan

240 **juggler** sorcerer

243 **took . . . as** pretended to be

245 **And . . . me** i.e., and blandly staring me down. (With
    wordplay on "face" and "outfacing.")

246 **possessed** mad.

Of vile confederates. Along with them
They brought one Pinch, a hungry, lean-faced villain,
A mere anatomy, a mountebank,   239
A threadbare juggler and a fortune-teller,   240
A needy, hollow-eyed, sharp-looking wretch,
A living dead man. This pernicious slave,
Forsooth, took on him as a conjurer   243
And, gazing in mine eyes, feeling my pulse,
And with no face, as 'twere, outfacing me,   245
Cries out I was possessed. Then all together   246
They fell upon me, bound me, bore me thence,
And in a dark and dankish vault at home
There left me and my man, both bound together,
Till, gnawing with my teeth my bonds in sunder,
I gained my freedom and immediately
Ran hither to Your Grace, whom I beseech
To give me ample satisfaction
For these deep shames and great indignities.

ANGELO
　　My lord, in truth, thus far I witness with him,
　　That he dined not at home but was locked out.

DUKE
　　But had he such a chain of thee, or no?

ANGELO
　　He had, my lord, and when he ran in here
　　These people saw the chain about his neck.

SECOND MERCHANT [to E. Antipholus]
　　Besides, I will be sworn these ears of mine
　　Heard you confess you had the chain of him
　　After you first forswore it on the mart,
　　And thereupon I drew my sword on you;
　　And then you fled into this abbey here,
　　From whence, I think, you are come by miracle.

E. ANTIPHOLUS
　　I never came within these abbey walls,

270 **intricate impeach** involved accusation

271 **Circe's cup** the charmed cup, a draft of which turned men into beasts (as told in Homer's *Odyssey*).

273 **coldly** calmly, rationally.

282 **mated** stupefied

Nor ever didst thou draw thy sword on me.
I never saw the chain, so help me Heaven!
And this is false you burden me withal.

DUKE

Why, what an intricate impeach is this!   270
I think you all have drunk of Circe's cup.   271
If here you housed him, here he would have been.
If he were mad, he would not plead so coldly.   273
[To Adriana] You say he dined at home; the goldsmith here
Denies that saying. [To E. Dromio] Sirrah, what say you?

E. DROMIO

Sir, he dined with her there, at the Porcupine.

COURTESAN

He did, and from my finger snatched that ring.

E. ANTIPHOLUS

'Tis true, my liege. This ring I had of her.

DUKE [to the Courtesan]

Saw'st thou him enter at the abbey here?

COURTESAN

As sure, my liege, as I do see Your Grace.

DUKE

Why, this is strange. Go call the Abbess hither.
I think you are all mated or stark mad.   282

                              Exit one to the Abbess.

EGEON

Most mighty Duke, vouchsafe me speak a word.
Haply I see a friend will save my life
And pay the sum that may deliver me.

DUKE

Speak freely, Syracusian, what thou wilt.

EGEON [to E. Antipholus]

Is not your name, sir, called Antipholus?
And is not that your bondman, Dromio?

299 **careful** care-filled

300 **defeatures** disfigurements, blemishes

311 **my . . . cares** my voice enfeebled by discordant cares.

312 **grainèd** lined, furrowed

313 **In . . . snow** i.e., by my white hairs, that have dried up
the sap of my youth

E. DROMIO

> Within this hour I was his bondman, sir,
> But he, I thank him, gnawed in two my cords.
> Now am I Dromio and his man, unbound.

EGEON

> I am sure you both of you remember me.

E. DROMIO

> Ourselves we do remember, sir, by you;
> For lately we were bound, as you are now.
> You are not Pinch's patient, are you, sir?

EGEON

> Why look you strange on me? You know me well.

E. ANTIPHOLUS

> I never saw you in my life till now.

EGEON

> Oh, grief hath changed me since you saw me last,
> And careful hours with Time's deformèd hand   299
> Have written strange defeatures in my face.   300
> But tell me yet, dost thou not know my voice?

E. ANTIPHOLUS   Neither.

EGEON   Dromio, nor thou?

E. DROMIO   No, trust me, sir, nor I.

EGEON   I am sure thou dost.

E. DROMIO   Ay, sir, but I am sure I do not; and whatsoever a man denies, you are now bound to believe him.

EGEON

> Not know my voice! O time's extremity,
> Hast thou so cracked and splitted my poor tongue
> In seven short years, that here my only son
> Knows not my feeble key of untuned cares?   311
> Though now this grainèd face of mine be hid   312
> In sap-consuming winter's drizzled snow   313
> And all the conduits of my blood froze up,
> Yet hath my night of life some memory,

316 **wasting lamps** i.e., dimming eyes
321 **But** Only
333 **genius** attendant spirit
335 **deciphers** distinguishes

My wasting lamps some fading glimmer left,   316
My dull deaf ears a little use to hear.
All these old witnesses—I cannot err—
Tell me thou art my son Antipholus.

E. ANTIPHOLUS
I never saw my father in my life.

EGEON
But seven years since, in Syracusa, boy,   321
Thou know'st we parted. But perhaps, my son,
Thou sham'st to acknowledge me in misery.

E. ANTIPHOLUS
The Duke and all that know me in the city
Can witness with me that it is not so.
I ne'er saw Syracusa in my life.

DUKE
I tell thee, Syracusian, twenty years
Have I been patron to Antipholus,
During which time he ne'er saw Syracusa.
I see thy age and dangers make thee dote.

> *Enter the Abbess, with Antipholus and Dromio of*
> *Syracuse.*

ABBESS
Most mighty Duke, behold a man much wronged.

> *All gather to see them.*

ADRIANA
I see two husbands, or mine eyes deceive me.

DUKE
One of these men is genius to the other;   333
And so of these, which is the natural man,
And which the spirit? Who deciphers them?   335

S. DROMIO
I, sir, am Dromio. Command him away.

344 **burden** birth

352 **rude** rough, simple

357 **his morning story** i.e., the history Egeon related this
morning

359 **semblance** appearance

360 **urging** urgent account

E. DROMIO
I, sir, am Dromio. Pray, let me stay.

S. ANTIPHOLUS
Egeon art thou not? Or else his ghost?

S. DROMIO
Oh, my old master! Who hath bound him here?

ABBESS
Whoever bound him, I will loose his bonds
And gain a husband by his liberty.
Speak, old Egeon, if thou be'st the man
That hadst a wife once called Emilia
That bore thee at a burden two fair sons.   344
Oh, if thou be'st the same Egeon, speak,
And speak unto the same Emilia!

EGEON
If I dream not, thou art Emilia.
If thou art she, tell me where is that son
That floated with thee on the fatal raft?

ABBESS
By men of Epidamnum he and I
And the twin Dromio all were taken up;
But by and by rude fishermen of Corinth   352
By force took Dromio and my son from them,
And me they left with those of Epidamnum.
What then became of them I cannot tell;
I to this fortune that you see me in.

DUKE
Why, here begins his morning story right: 357
These two Antipholus', these two so like,
And these two Dromios, one in semblance—   359
Besides her urging of her wreck at sea—   360
These are the parents to these children,
Which accidentally are met together.
Antipholus, thou cam'st from Corinth first?

376 **leisure** opportunity

S. ANTIPHOLUS
No, sir, not I. I came from Syracuse.

DUKE
Stay, stand apart. I know not which is which.

E. ANTIPHOLUS
I came from Corinth, my most gracious lord—

E. DROMIO   And I with him.

E. ANTIPHOLUS
Brought to this town by that most famous warrior,
Duke Menaphon, your most renownèd uncle.

ADRIANA
Which of you two did dine with me today?

S. ANTIPHOLUS
I, gentle mistress.

ADRIANA   And are not you my husband?

E. ANTIPHOLUS   No, I say nay to that.

S. ANTIPHOLUS
And so do I. Yet did she call me so,
And this fair gentlewoman, her sister here,
Did call me brother. [*To Luciana*] What I told you then
I hope I shall have leisure to make good,   376
If this be not a dream I see and hear.

ANGELO [*pointing to the chain Antipholus of Syracuse wears*]
That is the chain, sir, which you had of me.

S. ANTIPHOLUS
I think it be, sir. I deny it not.

E. ANTIPHOLUS [*to Angelo*]
And you, sir, for this chain arrested me.

ANGELO
I think I did, sir. I deny it not.

ADRIANA [*to Antipholus of Ephesus*]
I sent you money, sir, to be your bail,
By Dromio, but I think he brought it not.

387 **still** continually

391 **life** pardon.

394 **vouchsafe** deign, agree

396 **at large** at length

398 **sympathizèd** shared in by all equally

405 **calendars . . . nativity** i.e., the Dromios, since the servants were born at the same time as their masters

406 **a gossips' feast** a christening feast, here to celebrate, belatedly, the start of life for the two sets of twins, who were not truly born till now; also, a feast of companionship

408 **gossip** i.e., be a hearty companion, take part

E. DROMIO   No, none by me.

S. ANTIPHOLUS [*showing his purse to Adriana*]
This purse of ducats I received from you,
And Dromio my man did bring them me.
I see we still did meet each other's man,   387
And I was ta'en for him, and he for me,
And thereupon these errors are arose.

E. ANTIPHOLUS [*offering money*]
These ducats pawn I for my father here.

DUKE
It shall not need. Thy father hath his life.   391

COURTESAN [*to E. Antipholus*]
Sir, I must have that diamond from you.

E. ANTIPHOLUS [*giving the ring*]
There, take it, and much thanks for my good cheer.

ABBESS
Renownèd Duke, vouchsafe to take the pains   394
To go with us into the abbey here
And hear at large discoursèd all our fortunes,   396
And all that are assembled in this place,
That by this sympathizèd one day's error   398
Have suffered wrong. Go, keep us company,
And we shall make full satisfaction.
Thirty-three years have I but gone in travail
Of you, my sons, and till this present hour
My heavy burden ne'er deliverèd.
The Duke, my husband, and my children both,
And you the calendars of their nativity,   405
Go to a gossips' feast, and joy with me;   406
After so long grief, such nativity!

DUKE
With all my heart I'll gossip at this feast.   408

>   *Exeunt omnes. Manent the two Dromios and two*
>   *brothers* [*Antipholus*].

411 **lay at host** were put up at the inn
416 **kitchened** entertained in the kitchen
417 **sister** sister-in-law
418 **glass** mirror
420 **gossiping** merrymaking.
423 **cuts** lots

S. DROMIO [*to Antipholus of Ephesus*]
  Master, shall I fetch your stuff from shipboard?

E. ANTIPHOLUS
  Dromio, what stuff of mine hast thou embarked?

S. DROMIO
  Your goods that lay at host, sir, in the Centaur.   411

S. ANTIPHOLUS
  He speaks to me.—I am your master, Dromio.
  Come, go with us. We'll look to that anon.
  Embrace thy brother there; rejoice with him.
                    Exeunt [*the two brothers Antipholus*].

S. DROMIO
  There is a fat friend at your master's house
  That kitchened me for you today at dinner.   416
  She now shall be my sister, not my wife.   417

E. DROMIO
  Methinks you are my glass and not my brother.   418
  I see by you I am a sweet-faced youth.
  Will you walk in to see their gossiping?   420

S. DROMIO   Not I, sir, you are my elder.

E. DROMIO   That's a question. How shall we try it?

S. DROMIO   We'll draw cuts for the senior. Till then, lead   423
  thou first.

E. DROMIO   Nay, then, thus:
  We came into the world like brother and brother,
  And now let's go hand in hand, not one before
      another.   *Exeunt.*

DATE AND TEXT

   The earliest known edition of *The Comedy of Errors* is in the
First Folio of 1623. Its first-mentioned production, however, was
on Innocents Day, December 28, 1594, when a "Comedy of
Errors (like to *Plautus* his *Menechmus*)" was performed by profes-
sional actors as part of the Christmas Revels at Gray's Inn (one
of the Inns of Court, where young men studied law) in London.
The evening's festivities are set down in *Gesta Grayorum*, a contemporary account of the revels, though not published until
1688. According to this record, the evening was marred by such
tumult and disorder that the invited guests from the Inner
Temple (another of the Inns of Court) refused to stay; thereafter,
the night became known as "The Night of Errors." References to
sorcery and enchantment in the play leave little doubt that it
was Shakespeare's.
   Some scholars argue that the play was not newly written for
this occasion. To them, the play seems early: slight in characterization, and full of punning wit reminiscent of *Love's Labor's Lost*
and *The Two Gentlemen of Verona*. Topical clues are suggestive
but not conclusive. Chief of these is the joke about France being
"armed and reverted, making war against her heir" (3.2.123–4).
Unquestionably, this refers to France's civil wars between Henry
of Navarre and his Catholic opposition. Since Henry became a
Catholic and the King of France in 1593, most scholars prefer a
date before 1593. Peter Alexander (*Shakespeare's Life and Art*,
1961) has even argued for a date prior to 1589, since Henry III
died in that year, leaving Henry of Navarre as nominal king
rather than heir. The sad truth is that we probably cannot attach too much weight to either conclusion. Allusions to the
French civil wars during the early 1590s were common but also
imprecise; the joke would have seemed relevant at almost any
time up to 1595. The same is probably true of the allusion to
Spain's sending "whole armadas of carracks" (3.2.135–6). This

is often taken to refer to the Spanish Armada, 1588, but may refer instead to the Portuguese *Madre de Dios*, captured and brought to England in 1592, or to a similar venture. In short, it is virtually impossible to prove that *The Comedy of Errors* precedes *Love's Labor's Lost*, *The Two Gentlemen of Verona*, or *The Taming of the Shrew*. Those scholars who think it unlikely that the young gentlemen of Gray's Inn would have bestowed their attention on a play already five years old prefer a date of 1594.

A lost play called *The History of Error* was acted before the Queen by the Children of Paul's (a company of boy actors from St. Paul's School) at Hampton Court on New Year's night, 1577. About this play we know nothing other than its suggestive title, and speculation that Shakespeare may have adapted it has been generally abandoned.

The Folio text, based probably on Shakespeare's own manuscript, is generally a good text, although, as is common in authorial manuscripts, the form of the characters' names frequently varies in the stage directions and speech prefixes. Perhaps a few performance-oriented annotations have been added to the authorial manuscript.

TEXTUAL NOTES

These textual notes are not a historical collation, either of the early folios or of more recent editions; they are simply a record of departure in this edition from the copy text. The reading adopted in this edition appears in boldface, followed by the rejected reading from the copy text, i.e., the First Folio. Changes in lineation are not indicated, nor are some minor and obvious typographical errors.

Copy text: the First Folio. Scene divisions not marked in the Folio are provided at 1.2, 2.2, 3.2, 4.2, 4.3, and 4.4.

1.1. 0.2 [and elsewhere] **Syracuse** *Siracusa*   **1** [and elsewhere] EGEON *Marchant*   **41** [and throughout] **Epidamnum** *Epidamium*   **42 the** he   **102 upon** vp   **116 bark** backe   **123 thee** they   **151 health** helpe

1.2. 0.1 Antipholus [of Syracuse] *Antipholis Erotes*   **[First] Merchant** a *Marchant*   **1** [and elsewhere] FIRST MERCHANT *Mer.* [also called E. *Mar.*]   **4 arrival** a riuall   **15 travel** trauaile   **30** [and elsewhere] **lose** loose   **32 s.d. Exit** *Exeunt*   **40 unhappy** vnhappie a   **66 clock** cooke   **94.1 Exit** *Exeunt*

2.1. 0.1 Antipholus [of Ephesus] *Antipholis Sereptus*   **11 o' door** adore   **12 ill** thus   **45 two** too   **60 thousand** hundred   **63 come home** come   **71 errand** arrant   **106 o' love** a loue   **111 Wear** Where   **115.1 Exeunt** *Exit*

2.2. 0.1 Antipholus of Syracuse *Antipholus Errotis*   **6.1 of Syracuse** *Siracusia*   **12 didst** did didst   **14 s. ANTIPHOLUS** *E. Ant.*   **79 men** them   **97 tiring** trying   **101 e'en** in   **135 off** of   **174 stronger** stranger   **185 offered** free'd   **189 elves** Owles   **193 drone** *Dromio*   **194 not I** I not

3.1. 71 cake cake here   **75 you** your   **89 her** your   **91 her** your   **116** [and throughout] **Porcupine** *Porpentine*

3.2. 0.1 *Luciana* Iuliana   **1** LUCIANA *Iulia*   **4 building** buildings
ruinous ruinate   **16 attaint** attaine   **21 but** not   **26 wife** wise
46 sister's sister   **49 bed** bud   **them** thee   **57 where** when
109 and is   **126 chalky** chalkle   **136 carracks** Carrects
162 [and elsewhere] lest least

4.1. 1 [and elsewhere) SECOND MERCHANT *Mar.*   **7 [and elsewhere]**
ANGELO *Gold.*   **13.1 Enter . . . Ephesus** Enter Antipholus Ephes.
Dromio   **17 her** their   **28 carat** charect   **87 then** then sir

4.2. 6 Of Oh   **34 One** On   **48 That** Thus   **61 'a** I   **66 s.d.**
Exeunt Exit

4.3. 1 S. ANTIPHOLUS [not in F]   **58 if you** if   **78 s.d. Exeunt** Exit

4.4. 42 to prophesy the prophesie   **104 those** these   **106.1–2**
Enter . . . strives [after line 105 in F]   **113 his** this   **130.1–3** [after
line 131 in F] ***Manent*** Manet   **143.1–2 Enter . . . drawn** Enter
Antipholus Siracusia with his Rapier drawne, and Dromio Sirac.
146.1 Run all out [after "bound again" in line 146 in F]

5.1. 121 death depth   **155 whither** whether   **168** SERVANT [not in
F]   **175 scissors** Cizers   **180** SERVANT *Mess.*   **195** EGEON *Mar. Fat.*
283 EGEON *Fa.* [and elsewhere *Fath.* and *Father*]   **330.1–2**
Antipholus . . . Syracuse Antipholus Siracusa, and Dromio Sir.
357–62 [these lines follow line 346 in F]   **358 Antipholus'** Antipholus
403 ne'er are   **406 joy** go   **408.1 Manent** Manet   **414.1 Exeunt**
Exit

SHAKESPEARE'S SOURCES

The Comedy of Errors is based chiefly on the *Menaechmi* of Plautus (c. 254–184 B.C.). Shakespeare appears to have used the Latin, which was available to him in numerous Renaissance texts. He may also have known in manuscript the translation into English by "W. W." (? William Warner), published in 1595.

A full modernized text of the "W. W." translation of the *Menaechmi* follows. A comparison of it with Shakespeare's play suggests how much he has retained and what he has changed. In Plautus, the story concerns two separated twins, one of whom (Menaechmus the Traveler of Syracuse) has come by chance, accompanied by his servant, Messenio, to the city of Epidamnum, where his long-lost brother, Menaechmus the Citizen, lives. Menaechmus the Citizen, in the company of the parasite Peniculus, quarrels with his wife and arranges to lunch with the courtesan Erotium. The confusion begins when Menaechmus the Traveler is mistaken for his twin by Erotium's cook, Cylindrus, and then by Erotium herself, who invites him to lunch and to her bed. She bids him take a cloak (which Menaechmus the Citizen had given her that morning) to the dyer's for alteration. A short time later, Peniculus too mistakes Menaechmus the Traveler for the Epidamnian twin, upbraids him for having dined while the parasite was absent, and threatens to tell Menaechmus's wife of his carryings-on. Erotium's maid brings Menaechmus the Traveler a chain or bracelet to be mended at the goldsmith's. Menaechmus the Citizen now returns home from a busy day to a furious wife and a vindictive Peniculus. Among other matters the wife demands the return of her cloak, which, as she suspects, her husband stole from her and gave to Erotium. The husband, locked out of his own house by his angry wife, must now confront Erotium, who insists that she gave her chain and the cloak to him. The Citizen goes to seek the help of his friends. Menaechmus the Traveler shows up at this point and is angrily abused by the wife and by her father, both of whom consider the supposed husband to be mad. They send for a doctor, who arrives after Menaechmus the Traveler has fled; they instead detain Menaechmus the Citizen as a madman. Messenio the servant now returns to his supposed master and fights manfully with his master's captors. Finally the two twins confront one another and unravel the mystery.

Shakespeare creates the two Dromios in place of Messenio, plays down the role of the Courtesan, dignifies the part of the wife, invents the sympathetic role of Luciana her sister, eliminates the parasite and the wife's father, and replaces the Courtesan's maid and cook with comic servants such as Luce, or Nell, the kitchen-wench in the household of Antipholus of Ephesus. The conventional doctor, Medicus, becomes the zany Dr. Pinch. The setting is Ephesus rather than Epidamnum. Plautus's detached ironic tone and his matter-of-fact depiction of courtesans and parasites are replaced by a thematic emphasis on patience and loyalty in marriage. The name "Dromio" may have come from John Lyly's Mother Bombie.

The dual identity of the servants, and the superb confusion of act 3 when Antipholus of Ephesus is locked out of his own house, are derived in good part from Plautus's Amphitruo. In the relevant portion of that play, Amphitryon's wife, Alcmena, is courted by Jupiter disguised as her husband, while Mercury guards the door in the guise of Amphitryon's slave Sosia. The real Sosia approaches, but is so bewildered by Mercury's inventive wit that he begins to doubt his own identity. Later, at Jupiter's behest, Mercury again poses as Sosia to dupe Amphitryon and deny him entrance to his own house. Ultimately, after Alcmena has given birth to twins, one by Jupiter (Hercules) and one by Amphitryon (Iphiclus), Jupiter tells Amphitryon the truth.

The "framing" action of The Comedy of Errors, concerning old Egeon's painful separation from his wife and their eventual reunion, is derived not from Plautus but from the story of Apollonius of Tyre. Shakespeare later used this story for Pericles, and for that play his sources were chiefly two: the Confessio Amantis by John Gower, book 8, and Laurence Twine's The

Pattern of Painful Adventures, translated from a French version based in turn on a popular story in the *Gesta Romanorum*. Perhaps Shakespeare was acquainted with these same versions when he wrote *The Comedy of Errors*; in 1576 Twine's account was entered in the Stationers' Register, the official record book of the London Company of Stationers (booksellers and printers), although the earliest extant edition dates from around 1594–1595. Gower's account had been printed by William Caxton (England's first printer) in 1493 and reprinted in 1532 and 1554.

In Gower's *Confessio*, Apollonius's wife Lucina gives birth to a daughter on board ship and, having apparently died in childbirth, is put into a chest and committed to the sea. Washing ashore at Ephesus, she is restored by the physician Cerimon. She becomes a priestess in the Temple of Diana. Years later, Apollonius comes to Ephesus, is first reunited with his daughter Thais, and then is told in a vision to go to the Temple. There he discovers the "Abbess" to be his long-lost wife. Shakespeare has added the threatened hanging from which Egeon is finally rescued.

MENAECHMI

By *Plautus*
Translated by William Warner (?)

[*Dramatis personae*

MENAECHMUS THE CITIZEN, *residing in Epidamnum*
MENAECHMUS THE TRAVELER, *his twin, also called Sosicles*
MESSENIO, *bondslave of Menaechmus the Traveler*
PENICULUS, *parasite attached to Menaechmus the Citizen*
MULIER, *wife of Menaechmus the Citizen*
EROTIUM, *a courtesan*
CYLINDRUS, *her cook*
ANCILLA, *her maid*
SENEX, *Mulier's father*

MEDICUS, *a doctor*

SAILORS

SCENE: *A street in Epidamnum, on which are facing the houses*
of Menaechmus the Citizen and Erotium the courtesan]

The Argument

Two twinborn sons a Sicil merchant had:
    Menaechmus one and Sosicles the other.
The first his father lost a little lad;
    The grandsire named the latter like his brother.
This, grown a man, long travel took to seek
    His brother, and to Epidamnum came
Where th' other dwelt enriched, and him so like
    That citizens there take him for the same.
Father, wife, neighbors each mistaking either,
Much pleasant error ere they meet together.

I.I   *Enter Peniculus, a parasite.*

PENICULUS Peniculus was given me for my name[1] when I was
young, because like a broom I swept all clean away wheresoe'er I
be come: namely, all the victuals which are set before me. Now,
in my judgment men that clap iron bolts on such captives as
they would keep safe and tie those servants in chains who they
think will run away, they commit an exceeding great folly. My
reason is, these poor wretches enduring one misery upon another never cease devising how, by wrenching asunder their
gyves[2] or by some subtlety or other, they may escape such cursed
bonds. If then ye would keep a man without all suspicion of running away from ye, the surest way is to tie him with meat, drink,
and ease; let him ever be idle, eat his bellyful, and carouse while
his skin will hold, and he shall never, I warrant ye, stir a foot.
These strings to tie one by the teeth pass all the bonds of iron,
steel, or what metal soever, for the more slack and easy ye make
them, the faster still they tie the party which is in them. I speak this
upon experience of myself, who am now going for Menaechmus,

1.1   **1 for my name** (*Peniculus* in Latin means "brush for removing
dirt.")   **2 gyves** fetters

there willingly to be tied to his good cheer. He is commonly so exceeding bountiful and liberal in his fare, as no marvel though such guests as myself be drawn to his table and tied there in his dishes. Now, because I have lately been a stranger there, I mean to visit him at dinner, for my stomach methinks even thrusts me into the fetters of his dainty fare. But yonder I see his door open and himself ready to come forth.

1.2   *Enter Menaechmus [the Citizen, from his house], talking back to his wife within.*

MENAECHMUS THE CITIZEN   If ye were not such a brabbling[1] fool and madbrain scold as ye are, ye would never thus cross your husband in all his actions! [*To himself*] 'Tis no matter. Let her serve me thus once more, I'll send her home to her dad with a vengeance. I can never go forth a-doors but she asketh me whither I go, what I do, what business, what I fetch, what I carry, as though she were a constable or a toll-gatherer. I have pampered her too much. She hath servants about her, wool, flax, and all things necessary to busy her withal,[2] yet she watcheth and wondereth whither I go. Well, sith[3] it is so, she shall now have some cause. I mean to dine this day abroad with a sweet friend of mine.

PENICULUS [*aside*]   Yea, marry, now comes he to the point that pricks me. This last speech galls me as much as it would do his wife. If he dine not at home, I am dressed.[4]

MENAECHMUS THE CITIZEN [*to himself*]   We that have loves abroad and wives at home are miserably hampered. Yet, would every man could tame his shrew as well as I do mine! I have now filched away a fine riding cloak of my wife's which I mean to bestow upon one that I love better. Nay, if she be so wary and watchful over me, I count it an alms deed[5] to deceive her.

PENICULUS [*advancing*]   Come, what share have I in that same?

MENAECHMUS THE CITIZEN   Out, alas, I am taken.

PENICULUS   True, but by your friend.

MENAECHMUS THE CITIZEN   What, mine own Peniculus?

1.2   **1 brabbling** brawling (also in 4.1)   **2 withal** with   **3 sith** since   **4 dressed** treated with severity.   **5 an alms deed** a deed of charity

PENICULUS   Yours, i' faith, body and goods—if I had any.

MENAECHMUS THE CITIZEN   Why, thou hast a body.

PENICULUS   Yea, but neither goods nor good body.

MENAECHMUS THE CITIZEN   Thou couldst never come fitter in all
thy life.

PENICULUS   Tush, I ever do so to my friends. I know how to come
always in the nick. Where dine ye today?

MENAECHMUS THE CITIZEN   I'll tell thee of a notable prank.

PENICULUS   What, did the cook mar your meat in the dressing?[6]
Would I might see the reversion.[7]

MENAECHMUS THE CITIZEN   Tell me, didst thou see a picture how
Jupiter's eagle snatched away Ganymede, or how Venus stole
away Adonis?[8]

PENICULUS   Often, but what care I for shadows? I want substance.

MENAECHMUS THE CITIZEN   [showing a cloak he has concealed] Look
thee here. Look not I like such a picture?

PENICULUS   Oho, what cloak have ye got here?

MENAECHMUS THE CITIZEN   Prithee, say I am now a brave[9] fellow.

PENICULUS   But hark ye, where shall we dine?

MENAECHMUS THE CITIZEN   Tush, say as I bid thee, man.

PENICULUS   Out of doubt ye are a fine man.

MENAECHMUS THE CITIZEN   What? Canst add nothing of thine
own?

PENICULUS   Ye are a most pleasant gentleman.

MENAECHMUS THE CITIZEN   On, yet.

PENICULUS   Nay, not a word more, unless ye tell me how you and
your wife be fallen out.

MENAECHMUS THE CITIZEN   Nay, I have a greater secret than that
to impart to thee.

PENICULUS   Say your mind.

MENAECHMUS THE CITIZEN   Come farther this way from my house.

PENICULUS   [as they move away from the house] So, let me hear.

MENAECHMUS THE CITIZEN   Nay, farther yet.

PENICULUS   I warrant ye, man.

MENAECHMUS THE CITIZEN   Nay, yet farther.

6 dressing preparing.   7 reversion leftovers.   8 Jupiter's . . . Adonis
(Menaechmus the Citizen compares his stealth in stealing his wife's
cloak with the stealth used by the gods in their amours with mortals.)
9 brave fine

PENICULUS   'Tis pity ye were not made a waterman, to row in a wherry.[10]

MENAECHMUS THE CITIZEN   Why?

PENICULUS   Because ye go one way and look another still, lest your wife should follow ye. But what's the matter, is 't not almost dinnertime?

MENAECHMUS THE CITIZEN   See'st thou this cloak?

PENICULUS   Not yet. Well, what of it?

MENAECHMUS THE CITIZEN   This same I mean to give to Erotium.

PENICULUS   That's well, but what of all this?

MENAECHMUS THE CITIZEN   There I mean to have a delicious dinner prepared for her and me.

PENICULUS   And me?

MENAECHMUS THE CITIZEN   And thee.

PENICULUS   Oh, sweet word! What, shall I knock presently at her door?

MENAECHMUS THE CITIZEN   Ay, knock. But stay too, Peniculus; let's not be too rash. Oh, see, she is in good time coming forth.

PENICULUS   Ah, he now looks against[11] the sun. How her beams dazzle his eyes!

Enter Erotium [from her house].

EROTIUM   What, mine own Menaechmus? Welcome, sweetheart.

PENICULUS   And what, am I welcome too?

EROTIUM   You, sir? Ye are out of the number of my welcome guests.

PENICULUS   I am like a voluntary soldier—out of pay.

MENAECHMUS THE CITIZEN   Erotium, I have determined that here shall be pitched a field[12] this day. We mean to drink, for the heavens,[13] and which of us performs the bravest service at his weapon—the wine bowl—yourself as captain shall pay him his wages according to his deserts.

EROTIUM   Agreed.

PENICULUS   I would we had the weapons, for my valor pricks me to the battle.

---

10 **waterman . . . wherry** boatman plying his towboat for hire on a river.
11 **against** toward, into   12 **be pitched a field** a battle be fought
13 **for the heavens** i.e., by heaven (A mild oath.)

MENAECHMUS THE CITIZEN   Shall I tell thee, sweet mouse? I never
look upon thee but I am quite out of love with my wife.

EROTIUM   Yet ye cannot choose but ye must still wear something of
hers. What's this same? [*Indicating the cloak.*]

MENAECHMUS THE CITIZEN   This? Such a spoil,[14] sweetheart, I took
from her to put on thee.

EROTIUM   Mine own Menaechmus, well worthy to be my dear, of
all dearest!

PENICULUS [*aside*]   Now she shows herself in her likeness:[15] when
she finds him in the giving vein, she draws close to him.

MENAECHMUS THE CITIZEN   I think Hercules got not the garter
from Hippolyta so hardly[16] as I got this from my wife. Take this,
and with the same take my heart.   [*He gives her the cloak.*]

PENICULUS   Thus they must do that are right[17] lovers—[*aside*] especially if they mean to be beggars with any speed.[18]

MENAECHMUS THE CITIZEN   I bought this same of late[19] for my
wife. It stood me, I think, in[20] some ten pound.

PENICULUS [*aside*] There's ten pound bestowed very thriftily.

MENAECHMUS THE CITIZEN   But know ye what I would have ye do?

EROTIUM   It shall be done. Your dinner shall be ready.

MENAECHMUS THE CITIZEN   Let a good dinner be made for us three.
Hark ye: some oysters, a marrowbone pie or two, some arti-
chokes, and potato roots;[21] let our other dishes be as you please.

EROTIUM   You shall, sir.

MENAECHMUS THE CITIZEN   I have a little business in this city; by
that time dinner will be prepared. Farewell till then, sweet
Erotium. Come, Peniculus.

PENICULUS   Nay, I mean to follow ye. I will sooner leese[22] my life
than sight of you till this dinner be done.

                                    Exeunt [*Menaechmus and Peniculus*].

---

14 spoil booty   **15 in her likeness** i.e., in her true colors   **16 so
hardly** with as much difficulty. (One of Hercules' twelve labors was to
defeat the Amazons in battle and to obtain the girdle—here called a
garter—of their Queen Hippolyta.)   **17 right** true   **18 speed** success.
19 of late lately   **20 stood me . . . in** cost me   **21 potato roots**
potatoes   **22 leese** lose

EROTIUM [*calling into her house*]   Who's there? Call me Cylindrus the cook hither.

> *Enter Cylindrus.*

Cylindrus, take the handbasket, and here, there's ten shillings, is there not?

> [*Giving a handbasket and money.*]

CYCLINDRUS   'Tis so, mistress.

EROTIUM   Buy me of all the daintiest[23] meats ye can get—ye know what I mean—so as three may dine passing[24] well and yet no more than enough.

CYLINDRUS   What guests have ye today, mistress?

EROTIUM   Here will be Menaechmus and his parasite, and myself.

CYLINDRUS   That's ten persons in all.

EROTIUM   How many?

CYLINDRUS   Ten, for I warrant you that parasite may stand for eight at his victuals.

EROTIUM   Go, dispatch as I bid you, and look ye return with all speed.

CYLINDRUS   I will have all ready with a trice.   *Exeunt* [*separately*].

2.1   *Enter Menaechmus Sosicles* [*the Traveler*],
      Messenio his servant, and some sailors.

MENAECHMUS THE TRAVELER   Surely, Messenio, I think seafarers never take so comfortable a joy in anything as, when they have been long tossed and turmoiled in the wide seas, they hap at last to ken land.[1]

MESSENIO   I'll be sworn, I should not be gladder to see a whole country of mine own than I have been at such a sight. But, I pray, wherefore are we now come to Epidamnum? Must we needs go to see every town that we hear of?

MENAECHMUS THE TRAVELER   Till I find my brother, all towns are alike to me. I must try in all places.

---

23 **daintiest** choicest   24 **passing** surpassing, very
2.1 1 **hap . . . land** happen finally to catch sight of land.

MESSENIO   Why, then, let's even as long as we live seek your brother. Six years now have we roamed about thus—Istria, Hispania, Massilia, Illyria, all the Upper Sea, all high Greece, all haven[2] towns in Italy. I think if we had sought a needle all this time we must needs have found it, had it been above ground. It cannot be that he is alive; and to seek a dead man thus among the living, what folly is it?

MENAECHMUS THE TRAVELER   Yea, could I but once find any man that could certainly inform me of his death, I were satisfied. Otherwise I can never desist seeking. Little knowest thou, Messenio, how near my heart it goes.

MESSENIO   This is washing of a blackamoor.[3] Faith, let's go home, unless ye mean we should write a story of our travel.

MENAECHMUS THE TRAVELER   Sirrah, no more of these saucy speeches. I perceive I must teach ye how to serve me, not to rule me.

MESSENIO   Ay, so, now it appears what it is to be a servant. Well, yet I must speak my conscience. Do ye hear, sir? Faith, I must tell ye one thing: when I look into the lean estate of your purse and consider advisedly of your decaying stock, I hold it very needful to be drawing homeward, lest in looking for your brother we quite lose ourselves. For, this assure yourself: this town Epidamnum is a place of outrageous expenses, exceeding in all riot and lasciviousness and, I hear, as full of ribalds,[4] parasites, drunkards, catchpoles, coneycatchers,[5] and sycophants as it can hold. Then, for courtesans, why, here's the currentest stamp[6] of them in the world. Ye must not think here to scape with as light cost as in other places. The very name shows the nature: no man comes here *sine damno*.[7]

MENAECHMUS THE TRAVELER   Ye say very well indeed. Give me my purse into mine own keeping, because I will so be the safer, *sine damno*.

MESSENIO   Why, sir?

---

2 haven port   **3 washing of a blackamoor** i.e., performing an impossible task.   **4 ribalds** rascals   **5 catchpoles, coneycatchers** petty officers of justice and swindlers (both terms of contempt)   **6 currentest stamp** most current fashion   **7 *sine damno*** without being condemned (with a wordplay on Epi*damnum*).

MENAECHMUS THE TRAVELER Because I fear you will be busy among the* courtesans and so be cozened[8] of it. Then should I take great pains in belaboring your shoulders. So, to avoid both these harms, I'll keep it myself. [*He takes the purse.*]

MESSENIO I pray do so, sir. All the better.

Enter Cylindrus [with a handbasket].

CYLINDRUS [*to himself*] I have tickling gear[9] here, i' faith, for their dinners. It grieves me to the heart to think how that cormorant[10] knave Peniculus must have his share in these dainty morsels. But what? Is Menaechmus come already, before I could come from the market?—Menaechmus, how do ye, sir? How haps it ye come so soon?

MENAECHMUS THE TRAVELER God-a-mercy, my good friend, dost thou know me?

CYLINDRUS Know ye? No, not I. Where's Moldychaps that must dine with ye? A murrain[11] on his manners!

MENAECHMUS THE TRAVELER Whom meanest thou, good fellow?

CYLINDRUS Why, Peniculus, worship,[12] that whoreson lick-trencher,[13] your parasitical attendant.

MENAECHMUS THE TRAVELER What Peniculus? What attendant? My attendant?—Surely this fellow is mad.

MESSENIO Did I not tell ye what coneycatching villains ye should find here?

CYLINDRUS Menaechmus, hark ye, sir: ye come too soon back again to dinner. I am but returned from the market.

MENAECHMUS THE TRAVELER Fellow, here, thou shalt have money of me. [*He offers money.*] Go, get the priest to sacrifice for thee. I know thou art mad, else thou wouldst never use a stranger thus.

CYLINDRUS Alas, sir, Cylindrus was wont to be no stranger to you. Know ye not Cylindrus?

MENAECHMUS THE TRAVELER Cylindrus or Coliendrus[14] or what the devil thou art I know not; neither do I care to know.

---

8 cozened cheated (also in 3.1)   **9 tickling gear** delicate fare   **10 cormorant** i.e., devouring (like the large seabird)   **11 murrain** plague   **12 worship** i.e., your worship, your honor   **13 whoreson lick-trencher** i.e., good-for-nothing lick-platter or parasite   **14 Coliendrus** (Menaechmus the Traveler distorts the name so that it sounds like a word meaning "testicle.")

CYLINDRUS   I know you to be Menaechmus.

MENAECHMUS THE TRAVELER   Thou shouldst be in thy wits, in
that thou namest me so right. But tell me, where hast thou
known me?

CYLINDRUS   Where? Even here, where ye first fell in love with my
mistress, Erotium.

MENAECHMUS THE TRAVELER   I neither have lover, neither know I
who thou art.

CYLINDRUS   Know ye not who I am? Who fills your cup and dresses
your meat at our house?

MESSENIO   What a slave is this? That[15] I had somewhat to break
the rascal's pate withal![16]

MENAECHMUS THE TRAVELER   At your house, whenas I never came
in Epidamnum till this day?

CYLINDRUS   Oh, that's true. Do ye not dwell in yonder house?

> [Indicating the house of Menaechmus
> the Citizen.]

MENAECHMUS THE TRAVELER   Foul shame light upon them that
dwell there, for my part!

CYLINDRUS   Questionless he is mad indeed, to curse himself
thus.—Hark ye, Menaechmus.

MENAECHMUS THE TRAVELER   What say'st thou?

CYLINDRUS   If I may advise ye, ye shall bestow this money which ye
offered me upon a sacrifice for yourself, for out of doubt you are
mad that curse yourself.

MESSENIO   What a varlet art thou to trouble us thus?

CYLINDRUS   Tush, he will many times jest with me thus. Yet, when
his wife is not by, 'tis a ridiculous jest.

MENAECHMUS THE TRAVELER   What's that?

CYLINDRUS   This I say: think ye I have brought meat enough for
three of you? If not, I'll fetch more for you and your wench, and
Snatchcrust your parasite.

MENAECHMUS THE TRAVELER   What wenches? What parasites?

MESSENIO [to Cylindrus]   Villain, I'll make thee tell me what thou
meanest by all this talk!

---

15 That Would that   **16 break . . . withal** beat the rascal over the
head with.

CYLINDRUS   Away, jackanapes![17] I say nothing to thee, for I know thee not. I speak to him that I know.

MENAECHMUS THE TRAVELER   Out, drunken fool! Without doubt thou art out of thy wits.

CYLINDRUS   That you shall see by the dressing of your meat. Go, go, ye were better to go in and find somewhat to do there whiles your dinner is making ready. I'll tell my mistress ye be here.

[Exit to the Courtesan's.]

MENAECHMUS THE TRAVELER   Is he gone? Messenio, I think upon thy words already.

MESSENIO   Tush, mark, I pray. I'll lay[18] forty pound here dwells some courtesan to whom this fellow belongs.*

MENAECHMUS THE TRAVELER   But I wonder how he knows my name.

MESSENIO   Oh, I'll tell ye. These courtesans, as soon as any strange ship arriveth at the haven, they send a boy or a wench to inquire what they be, what their names be, whence they come, wherefore they come, etc. If they can by any means strike acquaintance with him, or allure him to their houses, he is their own. We are here in a tickle[19] place, master; 'tis best to be circumspect.

MENAECHMUS THE TRAVELER   I mislike not thy counsel, Messenio.

MESSENIO   Ay, but follow it, then. Soft,[20] here comes somebody forth. [To the sailors, giving them money.] Here, sirs, mariners, keep this same amongst you.

Enter Erotium [from her house].

EROTIUM [calling within]   Let the door stand so. Away, it shall not be shut. Make haste within there, ho! Maids, look that all things be ready. Cover the board,[21] put fire under the perfuming pans, let all things be very handsome. Where is he that Cylindrus said stood without[22] here?—Oh, what mean you, sweetheart, that ye come not in? I trust you think yourself more welcome to this house than to your own, and great reason why you should do so. Your dinner and all things are ready as you willed. Will ye go sit down?

---

17 jackanapes tame monkey, i.e., coxcomb, ridiculous fellow.   18 lay bet   19 tickle risky   20 Soft i.e., Wait a moment   21 Cover the board Set the table   22 without outside the door

MENAECHMUS THE TRAVELER Whom doth this woman speak to?

EROTIUM Even to you, sir. To whom else should I speak?

MENAECHMUS THE TRAVELER Gentlewoman, ye are a stranger to me, and I marvel at your speeches.

EROTIUM Yea, sir, but such a stranger as I acknowledge ye for my best and dearest friend, and well you have deserved it.

MENAECHMUS THE TRAVELER Surely, Messenio, this woman is mad or drunk, that useth all this kindness to me upon so small acquaintance.

MESSENIO Tush, did not I tell ye right? These be but leaves which fall upon you now in comparison of the trees that will tumble on your neck shortly. I told ye here were silver-tongued hacksters.[23] But let me talk with her a little.— Gentlewoman, what acquaintance have you with this man? Where have you seen him?

EROTIUM Where he saw me, here in Epidamnum.

MESSENIO In Epidamnum? Who never till this day set his foot within the town?

EROTIUM Go, go, flouting jack.[24]—Menaechmus, what need all this? I pray, go in.

MENAECHMUS THE TRAVELER She also calls me by my name.

MESSENIO She smells your purse.

MENAECHMUS THE TRAVELER Messenio, come hither. Here, take my purse. [*He gives him his purse.*] I'll know whether she aim at me or my purse ere I go.

EROTIUM Will ye go in to dinner, sir?

MENAECHMUS THE TRAVELER A good motion.[25] Yea, and thanks with all my heart.

EROTIUM Never thank me for that which you commanded to be provided for yourself.

MENAECHMUS THE TRAVELER That I commanded?

EROTIUM Yea, for you and your parasite.

MENAECHMUS THE TRAVELER My parasite?

EROTIUM Peniculus, who came with you this morning when you brought me the cloak which you got from your wife.

MENAECHMUS THE TRAVELER A cloak that I brought you which I got from my wife?

EROTIUM Tush, what needeth all this jesting? Pray, leave off.

23 **hacksters** swaggering ruffians. 24 **flouting jack** jeering fellow.
25 **motion** proposal.

MENAECHMUS THE TRAVELER   Jest or earnest, this I tell ye for a
truth: I never had wife, neither have I nor never was in this
place till this instant. For only thus far am I come since I brake
my fast[26] in the ship.

EROTIUM   What ship do ye tell me of?

MESSENIO   Marry, I'll tell ye: an old rotten weather-beaten ship
that we have sailed up and down in this six years. Is 't not time to
be going homewards, think ye?

EROTIUM   Come, come, Menaechmus, I pray, leave this sporting
and go in.

MENAECHMUS THE TRAVELER   Well, gentlewoman, the truth is you
mistake my person. It is some other that you look for.

EROTIUM   Why, think ye I know ye not to be Menaechmus, the son
of Moschus, and have heard ye say ye were born at Syracuse,*
where Agathocles did reign, then Pythia, then Liparo, and now
Hiero?

MENAECHMUS THE TRAVELER   All this is true.

MESSENIO   Either she is a witch, or else she hath dwelt there and
knew ye there.

MENAECHMUS THE TRAVELER   I'll go in with her, Messenio; I'll see
further of this matter.

MESSENIO   Ye are cast away,[27] then.

MENAECHMUS THE TRAVELER   Why so? I warrant thee I can lose
nothing. Somewhat I shall gain—perhaps a good lodging during
my abode here. I'll dissemble with her another while.—Now,
when you please, let us go in. I made strange[28] with you because
of this fellow here, lest he should tell my wife of the cloak which
I gave you.

EROTIUM   Will ye stay any longer for your Peniculus, your parasite?

MENAECHMUS THE TRAVELER   Not I. I'll neither stay for him nor
have him let in if he do come.

EROTIUM   All the better. But sir, will ye do one thing for me?

MENAECHMUS THE TRAVELER   What is that?

EROTIUM   To bear that cloak which you gave me to the dyer's to
have it new trimmed and altered.

MENAECHMUS THE TRAVELER   Yea, that will be well, so my wife
shall not know it. Let me have it with me after dinner. I will

26 brake my fast broke my fast, dined   **27 cast away** ruined   **28
made strange** acted distant

but speak a word or two with this fellow and then I'll follow ye in.

[*Exit Erotium into her house.*]

Ho, Messenio, come aside. Go and provide for thyself and these shipboys in some inn, then look that after dinner you come hither for me.

MESSENIO   Ah, master, will ye be coneycatched thus willfully?

MENAECHMUS THE TRAVELER   Peace, foolish knave. See'st thou not what a sot she is? I shall cozen her, I warrant thee.

MESSENIO   Ay, master.

MENAECHMUS THE TRAVELER   Wilt thou be gone?

[*Exit to the Courtesan's.*]

MESSENIO   See, see, she hath him safe enough now. Thus he hath escaped a hundred pirates' hands at sea, and now one land-rover hath boarded him at first encounter.—Come away, fellows.

[*Exeunt Messenio and sailors.*]

3.1   *Enter Peniculus.*

PENICULUS   Twenty years, I think, and more have I played the knave, yet never played I the foolish knave as I have done this morning. I follow Menaechmus, and he goes to the hall where now the sessions are holden. There thrusting ourselves into the press of people, when I was in the midst of all the throng he gave me the slip, that I could nevermore set eye on him, and, I dare swear, came directly to dinner. That I would he that first devised these sessions were hanged, and all that ever came of him! 'Tis such a hindrance to men that have belly business in hand. If a man be not there at his call, they amerce[1] him with a vengeance. Men that have nothing else to do, that do neither bid any man nor are themselves bidden to dinner, such should come to sessions, not we that have these matters to look to. If it were so, I had not thus lost my dinner this day, which I think in my conscience he did even purposely cozen me of.* Yet I mean to go see. If I can but light upon the reversion, I may perhaps get my pennyworth's. But how now? Is this Menaechmus coming away from thence? Dinner done, and all dispatched? What execrable luck have I!

Enter Menaechmus the Traveler [from the Courtesan's, carrying a cloak].

3.1 1 amerce penalize, fine

MENAECHMUS THE TRAVELER [*calling back into the Courtesan's*]
Tush, I warrant ye, it shall be done as ye would wish. I'll have it
so altered and trimmed new that it shall by no means be known
again.

PENICULUS [*aside*] He carries the cloak to the dyer's, dinner done,
the wine drunk up, the parasite shut out-of-doors. Well, let me
live no longer but I'll revenge this injurious mockery. But first I'll
hearken awhile what he saith.

MENAECHMUS THE TRAVELER Good gods, whoever had such luck
as I? Such cheer, such a dinner, such kind entertainment! And,
for a farewell, this cloak, which I mean shall go with me.

PENICULUS [*aside*] He speaks so softly I cannot hear what he saith.
I am sure he is now flouting at me for the loss of my dinner.

MENAECHMUS THE TRAVELER She tells me how I gave it her and
stole it from my wife. When I perceived she was in an error,
though I know not how, I began to soothe[2] her and to everything
as she said. Meanwhile I fared well, and that a' free cost.

PENICULUS [*aside*] Well, I'll go talk with him.

[*He comes forward.*]

MENAECHMUS THE TRAVELER Who is this same that comes to me?

PENICULUS Oh, well met, ficklebrain, false and treacherous dealer,
crafty and unjust promise-breaker! How have I deserved you
should so give me the slip, come before and dispatch the dinner,
deal so badly with him that hath reverenced ye like a son?

MENAECHMUS THE TRAVELER Good fellow, what meanest thou by
these speeches? Rail not on me, unless thou intend'st to receive
a railer's hire.[3]

PENICULUS I have received the injury, sure I am, already.

MENAECHMUS THE TRAVELER Prithee, tell me, what is thy name?

PENICULUS Well, well, mock on, sir, mock on. Do ye not know my
name?

MENAECHMUS THE TRAVELER In troth, I never saw thee in all my
life, much less do I know thee.

PENICULUS Fie, awake, Menaechmus, awake! Ye oversleep yourself.

---

2 **soothe** corroborate, back up, encourage, humor   3 **hire** payment,
wage, reward.

MENAECHMUS THE TRAVELER   I am awake. I know what I say.

PENICULUS   Know you not Peniculus?

MENAECHMUS THE TRAVELER   Peniculus or Pediculus,[4] I know thee not.

PENICULUS   Did ye filch a cloak from your wife this morning and bring it hither to Erotium?

MENAECHMUS THE TRAVELER   Neither have I wife, neither gave I any cloak to Erotium, neither filched I any from anybody.

PENICULUS   Will ye deny that which you did in my company?

MENAECHMUS THE TRAVELER*   Wilt thou say I have done this in thy company?

PENICULUS   Will I say it? Yea, I will stand to it.

MENAECHMUS THE TRAVELER   Away, filthy mad drivel,[5] away! I will talk no longer with thee.

PENICULUS [aside]   Not a world of men shall stay me but I'll go tell his wife of all the whole matter, sith he is at this point[6] with me. I will make this same as unblessed a dinner as ever he ate. [Exit.]

MENAECHMUS THE TRAVELER   It makes me wonder to see how everyone that meets me cavils[7] thus with me. Wherefore comes forth the maid, now?

Enter Ancilla, Erotium's maid [from the Courtesan's].

ANCILLA [offering a gold chain]   Menaechmus, my mistress commends her heartily to you, and, seeing you go that way to the dyer's, she also desireth you to take this chain with you and put it to mending at the goldsmith's. She would have two or three ounces of gold more in it and the fashion amended.

MENAECHMUS THE TRAVELER [taking the chain]   Either this or anything else within my power, tell her, I am ready to accomplish.

ANCILLA   Do ye know this chain, sir?

MENAECHMUS THE TRAVELER   Yea, I know it to be gold.

ANCILLA   This is the same you once took out of your wife's casket.

MENAECHMUS THE TRAVELER   Who, did I?

ANCILLA   Have you forgotten?

MENAECHMUS THE TRAVELER   I never did it.

ANCILLA   Give it me again, then.

---

4 Pediculus pedant   **5 drivel** drudge, menial   **6 point** position, determination   **7 cavils** disputes, finds fault (also in 4.1)

MENAECHMUS THE TRAVELER   Tarry. Yes, I remember it. 'Tis it I gave[8] your mistress.

ANCILLA   Oh, are ye advised?[9]

MENAECHMUS THE TRAVELER   Where are the bracelets that I gave her likewise?

ANCILLA   I never knew of any.

MENAECHMUS THE TRAVELER   Faith, when I gave this, I gave them too.

ANCILLA   Well, sir, I'll tell her this shall be done?

MENAECHMUS THE TRAVELER   Ay, ay, tell her so. She shall have the cloak and this both together.

ANCILLA   I pray, Menaechmus, put a little jewel for my ear to making[10] for me. Ye know I am always ready to pleasure you.

MENAECHMUS THE TRAVELER   I will. Give me the gold; I'll pay for the workmanship.

ANCILLA   Lay out[11] for me. I'll pay it ye again.

MENAECHMUS THE TRAVELER   Alas, I have none now.

ANCILLA   When you have, will ye?

MENAECHMUS THE TRAVELER   I will. Go, bid your mistress make no doubt of these. I warrant her I'll make the best hand[12] I can of them.   [*Exit Ancilla.*]

Is she gone? Do not all the gods conspire to load me with good luck? Well, I see 'tis high time to get me out of these coasts,[13] lest all these matters should be lewd[14] devices to draw me into some snare. There shall my garland lie, because, if they seek me, they may think I am gone that way. [*He lays down his garland.*] I will now go see if I can find my man Messenio, that I may tell him how I have sped.[15]   [*Exit.*]

4.1   *Enter Mulier, the wife of Menaechmus the Citizen, and Peniculus.*

MULIER   Thinks he I will be made such a sot, and to be still his drudge, while he prowls and purloins all that I have to give his trulls?

---

8 **'Tis it I gave** This is the one I gave   9 **are ye advised?** have you considered?   10 **put . . . to making** have a little earring made   11 **Lay out** Provide it   12 **hand** deal   13 **these coasts** this territory   14 **lewd** wicked   15 **sped** succeeded.

PENICULUS Nay, hold your peace. We'll catch him in the nick.[1]
This way he came, in his garland, forsooth, bearing the cloak to
the dyer's. And see, I pray, where the garland lies. This way he is
gone. See, see, where he comes again now without the cloak.

MULIER What shall I now do?

PENICULUS What? That which ye ever do: bait him for life.[2]

MULIER Surely I think it best so.

PENICULUS Stay. We will stand aside a little; ye shall catch him
unawares.   [They stand aside.]

    Enter Menaechmus the Citizen.

MENAECHMUS THE CITIZEN It would make a man at his wit's end to
see how brabbling causes are handled yonder at the court. If a
poor man, never so honest, have a matter come to be scanned,[3]
there is he outfaced[4] and overlaid with countenance.[5] If a rich
man, never so vile a wretch, come to speak, there they are all
ready to favor his cause. What with facing out bad causes for the
oppressors and patronizing some just actions for the wronged,
the lawyers, they pocket up all the gains. For mine own part, I
come not away empty, though I have been kept long against my
will; for, taking in hand to dispatch a matter this morning for
one of my acquaintance, I was no sooner entered into it but his
adversaries laid so hard unto his charge and brought such matter
against him that, do what I could, I could not wind myself out[6]
till now. I am sore afraid Erotium thinks much unkindness in me
that I stayed so long; yet she will not be angry, considering the
gift I gave her today.

PENICULUS [to Mulier] How think ye by that?[7]

MULIER [to Peniculus] I think him a most vile wretch thus to abuse
me.

MENAECHMUS THE CITIZEN I will hie me thither.
                        [He starts for the Courtesan's.]

MULIER [coming forward] Yea, go, pilferer, go with shame enough!
Nobody sees your lewd dealings and vile thievery.

4.1 1 **the nick** the act. 2 **bait him for life** i.e., harass him within an
inch of his life. 3 **scanned** judged 4 **outfaced** brazenly contra-
dicted 5 **overlaid with countenance** crushed by a show of virtue.
6 **wind myself out** extricate myself 7 **How . . . that?** What do you
think of that?

MENAECHMUS THE CITIZEN   How now, wife, what ails* thee? What is the matter?

MULIER   Ask ye me what's the matter? Fie upon thee!

PENICULUS [to Mulier]   Are ye not in a fit of an ague, your pulses beat so sore? To him, I say.

MENAECHMUS THE CITIZEN   Pray, wife, why are ye so angry with me?

MULIER   Oh, you know not?

PENICULUS   He knows, but he would dissemble it.

MENAECHMUS THE CITIZEN   What is it?

MULIER   My cloak.

MENAECHMUS THE CITIZEN   Your cloak?

MULIER   My cloak, man. Why do ye blush?

PENICULUS   He cannot cloak his blushing.—Nay, I might not go to dinner with you, do ye remember?—To him, I say.

MENAECHMUS THE CITIZEN   Hold thy peace, Peniculus.

PENICULUS   Ha! Hold my peace? Look ye, he beckons on[8] me to hold my peace.

MENAECHMUS THE CITIZEN   I neither beckon nor wink on him.

MULIER   Out,[9] out, what a wretched life is this that I live!

MENAECHMUS THE CITIZEN   Why, what ails ye, woman?

MULIER   Are ye not ashamed to deny so confidently that which is apparent?

MENAECHMUS THE CITIZEN   I protest unto you before all the gods— is not this enough?—that I beckoned not on him.

PENICULUS   Oh, sir, this is another matter.—Touch him in[10] the former cause.

MENAECHMUS THE CITIZEN   What former cause?

PENICULUS   The cloak, man, the cloak! Fetch the cloak again from the dyer's.

MENAECHMUS THE CITIZEN   What cloak?

MULIER   Nay, I'll say no more, sith ye know nothing of your own doings.

MENAECHMUS THE CITIZEN   Tell me, wife, hath any of your servants abused you? Let me know.

MULIER   Tush, tush.

---

8 beckons on gestures to   **9 Out** (An exclamation of anger.)   **10 Touch him in** Ask him about

MENAECHMUS THE CITIZEN I would not have you to be thus disquieted.

MULIER Tush, tush.

MENAECHMUS THE CITIZEN You are fallen out with some of your friends.

MULIER Tush, tush.

MENAECHMUS THE CITIZEN Sure I am I have not offended you.

MULIER No, you have dealt very honestly.

MENAECHMUS THE CITIZEN Indeed, wife, I have deserved none of these words. Tell me, are ye not well?

PENICULUS [to Mulier] What, shall he flatter ye now?

MENAECHMUS THE CITIZEN I speak not to thee, knave.—Good wife, come hither.

MULIER Away, away! Keep your hands off.

PENICULUS So, bid me to dinner with you again, then slip away from me; when you have done, come forth bravely in your garland to flout me! Alas, you knew not me even now.

MENAECHMUS THE CITIZEN Why, ass, I neither have yet dined, nor came I there, since we were there together.

PENICULUS Whoever heard one so impudent? Did ye not meet me here even now and would make me believe I was mad, and said ye were a stranger and ye knew me not?

MENAECHMUS THE CITIZEN Of a truth, since we went together to the sessions hall I never returned till this very instant, as you two met me.

PENICULUS Go to,[11] go to, I know ye well enough. Did ye think I would not cry quittance[12] with you? Yes, faith, I have told your wife all.

MENAECHMUS THE CITIZEN What hast thou told her?

PENICULUS I cannot tell. Ask her.

MENAECHMUS THE CITIZEN Tell me, wife, what hath he told ye of me? Tell me, I say. What was it?

MULIER As though you knew not. My cloak is stolen from me.

MENAECHMUS THE CITIZEN Is your cloak stolen from ye?

MULIER Do ye ask me?

MENAECHMUS THE CITIZEN If I knew, I would not ask.

---

11 **Go to** (An expression of remonstrance.)   12 **cry quittance** declare myself even, get even

PENICULUS Oh, crafty companion![13] How he would shift the matter.—Come, come, deny it not. I tell ye, I have bewrayed[14] all.

MENAECHMUS THE CITIZEN What hast thou bewrayed?

MULIER Seeing ye will yield to nothing, be it never so manifest, hear me, and ye shall know in few words both the cause of my grief and what he hath told me. I say my cloak is stolen from me.

MENAECHMUS THE CITIZEN My cloak is stolen from me?

PENICULUS Look how he cavils.—She saith it is stolen from her.

MENAECHMUS THE CITIZEN I have nothing to say to thee.—I say, wife, tell me.

MULIER I tell ye my cloak is stolen out of my house.

MENAECHMUS THE CITIZEN Who stole it?

MULIER He knows best that carried it away.

MENAECHMUS THE CITIZEN Who was that?

MULIER Menaechmus.

MENAECHMUS THE CITIZEN 'Twas very ill done of him. What Menaechmus was that?

MULIER You.

MENAECHMUS THE CITIZEN I? Who will say so?

MULIER I will.

PENICULUS And I. And that you gave it to Erotium.

MENAECHMUS THE CITIZEN I gave it?

MULIER You.

PENICULUS You, you, you. Shall we fetch a kennel of beagles that may cry nothing but "You, you, you, you"? For we are weary of it.

MENAECHMUS THE CITIZEN Hear me one word, wife. I protest unto you, by all the gods, I gave it her not. Indeed, I lent it her to use awhile.

MULIER Faith, sir, I never give nor lend your apparel out-of-doors. Methinks ye might let me dispose of mine own garments as you do of yours. I pray, then, fetch it me home again.

MENAECHMUS THE CITIZEN You shall have it again without fail.

MULIER 'Tis best for you that I have. Otherwise think not to roost within these doors again.

PENICULUS [to Mulier] Hark ye, what say ye to me now, for bringing these matters to your knowledge?

---

13 companion fellow. (A term of contempt.) **14 bewrayed** exposed, revealed

MULIER   I say, when thou hast anything stolen from thee, come to
me and I will help thee to seek it. And so farewell.

[*Exit into her house.*]

PENICULUS   God-a-mercy for nothing! That can never be, for I
have nothing in the world worth the stealing. So, now with husband and wife and all I am clean out of favor. A mischief on ye
all!   *Exit.*

MENAECHMUS THE CITIZEN   My wife thinks she is notably revenged
on me, now she shuts me out-of-doors, as though I had not a better place to be welcome to. If she shut me out, I know who will
shut me in. Now will I entreat Erotium to let me have the cloak
again to stop my wife's mouth withal, and then will I provide a
better for her.—Ho, who is within there? Somebody tell Erotium
I must speak with her.

Enter Erotium [from her house].

EROTIUM   Who calls?

MENAECHMUS THE CITIZEN   Your friend more than his own.[15]

EROTIUM   Oh, Menaechmus, why stand ye here? Pray, come in.*

MENAECHMUS THE CITIZEN   Tarry. I must speak with ye here.

EROTIUM   Say your mind.

MENAECHMUS THE CITIZEN   Wot ye what? My wife knows all the
matter now, and my coming is to request you that I may have
again the cloak which I brought you that so I may appease her.
And, I promise you, I'll give ye another worth two of it.

EROTIUM   Why, I gave it you to carry to your dyer's, and my chain
likewise, to have it altered.

MENAECHMUS THE CITIZEN   Gave me the cloak and your chain? In
truth, I never saw ye since I left it here with you and so went to
the sessions, from whence I am but now returned.

EROTIUM   Ah, then, sir, I see you wrought a device to defraud me of
them both. Did I therefore put ye in trust? Well, well.

MENAECHMUS THE CITIZEN   To defraud ye? No, but I say my wife
hath intelligence of the matter.

EROTIUM   Why, sir, I asked them not; ye brought them me of your
own free motion. Now ye require them again, take them, make

15 more than his own (i.e., because I am out of sorts with myself).

sops of them![16] You and your wife together, think ye I esteem them or you either? Go, come to me again when I send for you.

MENAECHMUS THE CITIZEN What, so angry with me, sweet Erotium? Stay, I pray, stay.

EROTIUM Stay? Faith, sir, no. Think ye I will stay at your request?
[Exit into her house.]

MENAECHMUS THE CITIZEN What, gone in chafing,[17] and clapped to[18] the doors? Now I am every way shut out for a very benchwhistler;[19] neither shall I have entertainment here nor at home. I were best to go try some other friends and ask counsel what to do.   [Exit.]

5.1   Enter Menaechmus the Traveler [as from the city, carrying the cloak, and] Mulier [from the house of Menaechmus the Citizen].

MENAECHMUS THE TRAVELER [to himself] Most foolishly was I overseen[1] in giving my purse and money to Messenio, whom I can nowhere find. I fear he is fallen into some lewd company.

MULIER [to herself] I marvel that my husband comes not yet. But see where he is now, and brings my cloak with him.

MENAECHMUS THE TRAVELER [to himself] I muse[2] where the knave should be.

MULIER [to herself] I will go ring a peal through both his ears for this his dishonest behavior.—Oh, sir, ye are welcome home, with your thievery on your shoulders. Are ye not ashamed to let all the world see and speak of your lewdness?[3]

MENAECHMUS THE TRAVELER How now? What lacks[4] this woman?

MULIER Impudent beast, stand ye to question about it? For shame, hold thy peace.

MENAECHMUS THE TRAVELER What offense have I done, woman, that I should not speak to you?

MULIER Askest thou what offense? Oh, shameless boldness!

16 make sops of them i.e., do what you like with them. (A sop is a bit of bread soaked in wine.)   17 chafing fretting, angry   18 clapped to slammed shut   19 benchwhistler i.e., idle person   5.1 1 overseen imprudent   2 muse wonder   3 lewdness wickedness.   4 lacks i.e., ails

MENAECHMUS THE TRAVELER   Good woman, did ye never hear why
the Grecians termed Hecuba[5] to be a bitch?

MULIER   Never.

MENAECHMUS THE TRAVELER   Because she did as you do now: on
whomsoever she met withal she railed, and therefore well deserved that dogged name.

MULIER   These foul abuses and contumelies[6] I can never endure;
nay, rather will I live a widow's life to my dying day.

MENAECHMUS THE TRAVELER   What care I whether thou livest as a
widow or as a wife? This passeth,[7] that I meet with none but thus
they vex me with strange speeches.

MULIER   What strange speeches? I say I will surely live a widow's
life rather than suffer thy vile dealings.

MENAECHMUS THE TRAVELER   Prithee, for my part, live a widow till
the world's end if thou wilt.

MULIER   Even now thou denied'st that thou stolest it from me, and
now thou bringest it home openly in my sight. Art not ashamed?

MENAECHMUS THE TRAVELER   Woman, you are greatly to blame to
charge me with stealing of this cloak, which this day another
gave me to carry to be trimmed.

MULIER   Well, I will first complain to my father. [*Calling into her
house.*] Ho, boy! Who is within there?

[*Enter Boy.*]

Vecio, go run quickly to my father. Desire him of all love[8] to
come over quickly to my house.

[*Exit Boy.*]

I'll tell him first of your pranks. I hope he will not see me[9] thus
handled.

MENAECHMUS THE TRAVELER   What i' God's name meaneth this
madwoman thus to vex me?

MULIER   I am mad because I tell ye of your vile actions and lewd pil-
fering away my apparel and my jewels to carry to your filthy drabs.[10]

MENAECHMUS THE TRAVELER   For whom this woman taketh me I
know not. I know her as much as I know Hercules' wife's father.[11]

---

5 Hecuba (The widow of King Priam of Troy is portrayed as embittered
in Euripides' play *Hecuba* and elsewhere.)   **6 contumelies** insults   **7
passeth** exceeds, goes too far   **8 of all love** for love's sake   **9 see me**
i.e., stand idly by and see me   **10 drabs** sluts.   **11 Hercules' wife's father** Oeneus of Calydon, father of Deianira.

MULIER   Do ye not know me? That's well. I hope ye know my father. Here he comes. Look, do ye know him?

MENAECHMUS THE TRAVELER   As much as I knew Calchas of Troy.[12] Even him and thee I know both alike.

MULIER   Dost know neither of us both, me nor my father?

MENAECHMUS THE TRAVELER   Faith, nor thy grandfather neither.

MULIER   This is like the rest of your behavior.

Enter Senex.

SENEX [*to himself*]   Though bearing so great a burden as old age, I can make no great haste; yet, as I can, I will go to my daughter, who I know hath some earnest business with me that she sends in such haste, not telling the cause why I should come. But I durst lay a wager I can guess near the matter. I suppose it is some brabble between her husband and her. These young women that bring great dowries to their husbands are so masterful and obstinate that they will have their own wills in everything and make men servants to their weak affections. And young men, too, I must needs say, be naught nowadays. Well, I'll go see. But yonder methinks stands my daughter, and her husband too. Oh, 'tis even as I guessed.

MULIER   Father, ye are welcome.

[*She and her father stand apart from Menaechmus the Traveler.*]

SENEX   How now, daughter? What, is all well? Why is your husband so sad? Have ye been chiding? Tell me, which of you is in the fault?

MULIER   First, father, know that I have not any way misbehaved myself, but the truth is I can by no means endure this bad man, to die for it,[13] and therefore desire you to take me home to you again.

SENEX   What is the matter?

MULIER   He makes me a stale[14] and laughingstock to all the world.

SENEX   Who doth?

MULIER   This good husband here, to whom you married me.

SENEX   See, see, how oft have I warned you of falling out with your husband?

MULIER   I cannot avoid it, if he doth so foully abuse me.

---

12 Calchas of Troy a Greek priest and seer, father of Cressida.   **13 to die for it** if I should have to die for it   **14 stale** object of ridicule

SENEX   I always told ye you must bear with him, ye must let him alone, ye must not watch him nor dog him nor meddle with his courses in any sort.

MULIER   He haunts naughty harlots under my nose.

SENEX   He is the wiser,15 because he cannot be quiet16 at home.

MULIER   There he feasts and banquets and spends and spoils.17

SENEX   Would ye have your husband serve ye as your drudge? Ye will not let him make merry nor entertain his friends at home.

MULIER   Father, will ye take his part in these abuses and forsake me?

SENEX   Not so, daughter, but if I see cause, I will as well tell him of his duty.

MENAECHMUS THE TRAVELER [aside]   I would I were gone from this prating father and daughter.

SENEX   Hitherto I see not but he keeps ye well. Ye want nothing—apparel, money, servants, meat, drink, all things necessary. I fear there is fault in you.

MULIER   But he filcheth away my apparel and my jewels to give to his trulls.

SENEX   If he doth so, 'tis very ill done; if not, you do ill to say so.

MULIER   You may believe me, father, for there you may see my cloak, which now he hath fetched home again, and my chain, which he stole from me.

SENEX   Now will I go talk with him to know the truth. [He approaches Menaechmus the Traveler.] Tell me, Menaechmus, how is it that I hear such disorder in your life? Why are ye so sad, man? Wherein hath your wife offended you?

MENAECHMUS THE TRAVELER   Old man—what to call ye I know not—by high Jove* and by all the gods I swear unto you, whatsoever this woman here accuseth me to have stolen from her, it is utterly false and untrue, and if I ever set foot within her doors I wish the greatest misery in the world to light upon me.

SENEX   Why, fond18 man, art thou mad to deny that thou ever sett'st foot within thine own house where thou dwellest?

MENAECHMUS THE TRAVELER   Do I dwell in that house?

SENEX   Dost thou deny it?

MENAECHMUS THE TRAVELER   I do.

15 is the wiser i.e., chooses a sensible course   16 be quiet find quiet
17 spoils is extravagant.   18 fond foolish

SENEX   Hark ye, daughter, are ye removed[19] out of your house?

MULIER   Father, he useth you as he doth me. This life I have with him!

SENEX   Menaechmus, I pray, leave this fondness. Ye jest too perversely with your friends.

MENAECHMUS THE TRAVELER   Good old father, what, I pray, have you to do with me? Or why should this woman thus trouble me, with whom I have no dealings in the world?

MULIER   Father, mark, I pray, how his eyes sparkle. They roll in his head; his color goes and comes; he looks wildly. See, see.

MENAECHMUS THE TRAVELER [aside]   What? They say now I am mad. The best way for me is to feign myself mad indeed; so I shall be rid of them.

MULIER   Look how he stares about! Now he gapes.

SENEX   Come away, daughter. Come from him.

MENAECHMUS THE TRAVELER [feigning madness]   Bacchus, Apollo, Phoebus, do ye call me to come hunt in the woods with you? I see, I hear, I come, I fly, but I cannot get out of these fields. Here is an old mastiff bitch stands barking at me, and by her stands an old goat that bears false witness against many a poor man.

SENEX   Out upon him, Bedlam fool!

MENAECHMUS THE TRAVELER   Hark! Apollo commands me that I should rend out her eyes with a burning lamp.

MULIER   Oh, father, he threatens to pull out mine eyes!

MENAECHMUS THE TRAVELER   Good gods, these folk say I am mad, and doubtless they are mad themselves.

SENEX   Daughter!

MULIER   Here, father. What shall we do?

SENEX   What if I fetch my folks hither and have him carried in before he do any harm?

MENAECHMUS THE TRAVELER [aside]   How now? They will carry me in if I look not to myself. I were best to scare them better yet.— Dost thou bid me, Phoebus, to tear this dog in pieces with my nails? If I lay hold on him I will do thy commandment.

SENEX   Get thee into thy house, daughter. Away, quickly!

[Mulier exits into her house.]

19 **removed** moved

MENAECHMUS THE TRAVELER   She is gone.—Yea, Apollo, I will sacrifice this old beast unto thee; and, if thou commandest me, I
will cut his throat with that dagger that hangs at his girdle.

                          [He advances threateningly toward Senex.]

SENEX   Come not near me, sirrah.

MENAECHMUS THE TRAVELER   Yea, I will quarter[20] him and pull all
the bones out of his flesh. Then will I barrel up[21] his bowels.

SENEX   Sure I am sore afraid he will do some hurt.

MENAECHMUS THE TRAVELER   Many things thou commandest me,
Apollo. Wouldst thou have me harness up these wild horses and
then climb up into the chariot and so override this old stinking
toothless lion? So, now I am in the chariot, and I have hold of
the reins. Here is my whip. Hait![22] Come, ye wild jades, make a
hideous noise with your stamping. Hait, I say! Will ye not go?

SENEX   What, doth he threaten me with his horses?

MENAECHMUS THE TRAVELER   Hark, now, Apollo bids me ride over
him that stands there and kill him. How now? Who pulls me
down from my chariot by the hairs of my head? Oh, shall I not
fulfill Apollo's commandment?

SENEX   See, see, what a sharp disease this is, and how well he was
even now! I will fetch a physician straight, before he grow too
far into this rage.   *Exit.*

MENAECHMUS THE TRAVELER   Are they both gone now? I'll then
hie me away to my ship. 'Tis time to be gone from hence.   *Exit.*

    Enter Senex and Medicus [the doctor, following].

SENEX   My loins ache with sitting and mine eyes with looking
while I stay for yonder lazy physician. See now where the creep-
ing drawlatch[23] comes.

MEDICUS   What disease hath he, said you? Is it a lethargy or a lunacy, or melancholy, or dropsy?

SENEX   Wherefore, I pray, do I bring you, but that you should tell
me what it is and cure him of it?

MEDICUS   Fie, make no question of that. I'll cure him, I warrant ye.
Oh, here he comes. Stay, let us mark what he doth.

                                          [They stand aside.]

---

20 quarter cut in quarters, as one would a traitor or criminal   **21 barrel
up** pack up, stow away   **22 Hait** i.e., Giddap.   **23 drawlatch** thief

Enter Menaechmus the Citizen.

MENAECHMUS THE CITIZEN   Never in my life had I more overthwart[24] fortune in one day! And all by the villainy of this false
knave the parasite, my Ulysses,[25] that works such mischiefs against
me, his king. But let me live no longer but I'll be revenged upon
the life of him. His life? Nay, 'tis my life, for he lives by my meat
and drink. I'll utterly withdraw the slave's life from him. And
Erotium! She showeth plainly what she is, who, because I require
the cloak again to carry to my wife, saith I gave it her, and flatly
falls out with me. How unfortunate am I!

SENEX   Do ye hear him?

MEDICUS   He complains of his fortune.

SENEX   Go to him.

MEDICUS *[approaching Menaechmus the Citizen]*   Menaechmus, how
do ye, man? Why keep you not your cloak over your arm? It is
very hurtful to your disease. Keep ye warm, I pray.

MENAECHMUS THE CITIZEN   Why, hang thyself. What carest thou?

MEDICUS   Sir, can you smell anything?

MENAECHMUS THE CITIZEN   I smell a prating dolt of thee.

MEDICUS   Oh, I will have your head thoroughly purged.[26] Pray tell
me, Menaechmus, what use you to drink? White wine or claret?

MENAECHMUS THE CITIZEN   What the devil carest thou?

SENEX   Look. His fit now begins.

MENAECHMUS THE CITIZEN   Why dost not as well ask me whether I
eat bread, or cheese, or beef, or porridge, or birds that bear feathers, or fishes that have fins?

SENEX   See what idle talk he falleth into.

MEDICUS   Tarry, I will ask him further.—Menaechmus, tell me, be
not your eyes heavy and dull sometimes?

MENAECHMUS THE CITIZEN   What dost think I am, an owl?

MEDICUS   Do not your guts gripe[27] ye and croak in your belly?

MENAECHMUS THE CITIZEN   When I am hungry they do, else not.

MEDICUS   He speaks not like a madman in that.—Sleep ye soundly
all night?

---

24 overthwart perverse   **25 Ulysses** (This hero of the Trojan War was
famous for his cunning.)   **26 have . . . purged** i.e., use a purging medi-
cine to clear your brain.   **27 gripe** offend, distress

MENAECHMUS THE CITIZEN When I have paid my debts, I do. The mischief light on thee with all thy frivolous questions!

MEDICUS Oh, now he rageth upon those words. Take heed.

SENEX Oh, this is nothing to the rage he was in even now. He called his wife bitch, and all to naught.[28]

MENAECHMUS THE CITIZEN Did I?

SENEX Thou didst, mad fellow, and threaten'st to ride over me here with a chariot and horses, and to kill me and tear me in pieces. This thou didst. I know what I say.

MENAECHMUS THE CITIZEN I say thou stolest Jupiter's crown from his head, and thou wert whipped through the town for it, and that thou hast killed thy father and beaten thy mother. Do ye think I am so mad that I cannot devise as notable lies of you as you do of me?

SENEX Master Doctor, pray heartily, make speed to cure him. See ye not how mad he waxeth?

MEDICUS I'll tell ye, he shall be brought over to my house and there will I cure him.

SENEX Is that best?

MEDICUS What else? There I can order him as I list.[29]

SENEX Well, it shall be so.

MEDICUS Oh, sir, I will make ye take neesing[30] powder this twenty days.

MENAECHMUS THE CITIZEN I'll beat ye first with a bastinado[31] this thirty days.

MEDICUS Fetch men to carry him to my house.

SENEX How many will serve the turn?

MEDICUS Being no madder than he is now, four will serve.

SENEX I'll fetch them. Stay you with him, Master Doctor.

MEDICUS No, by my faith, I'll go home to make ready all things needful. Let your men bring him hither.

SENEX I go.   *Exeunt [Medicus and Senex].*

MENAECHMUS THE CITIZEN Are they both gone? Good gods, what meaneth this? These men say I am mad, who without doubt are mad themselves. I stir not, I fight not, I am not sick. I speak to them, I know them. Well, what were I now best to do? I would go home, but my wife shuts me forth o' doors. Erotium is as far

28 **all to naught** i.e., abused her vehemently.   29 **order . . . list** provide for him as I think best.   30 **neesing** sneezing   31 **bastinado** cudgel

out with me too. Even here I will rest me till the evening. [*He lies down.*] I hope by that time they will take pity on me.

Enter Messenio, the Traveler's servant.

MESSENIO   The proof of a good servant is to regard his master's business as well in his absence as in his presence, and I think him a very fool that is not careful as well for his ribs and shoulders as for his belly and throat. When I think upon the rewards of a sluggard, I am ever pricked[32] with a careful regard of my back and shoulders, for in truth I have no fancy to these blows, as many a one hath. Methinks it is no pleasure to a man to be basted[33] with a rope's end two or three hours together. I have provided yonder in the town for all our mariners, and safely bestowed all my master's trunks and fardels,[34] and am now coming to see if he be yet got forth of this dangerous gulf where, I fear me, he* is overplunged. Pray God he be not overwhelmed and past help ere I come!

Enter Senex, with four lorarii, porters.

SENEX [*to the porters*]   Before gods and men, I charge and command you, sirs, to execute with great care that which I appoint you. If ye love the safety of your own ribs and shoulders, then go take me up my son-in-law. Lay all hands upon him. Why stand ye still? What do ye doubt? I say, care not for his threatenings nor for any of his words. Take him up and bring him to the physician's house. I will go thither before.   *Exit.*

MENAECHMUS THE CITIZEN [*as the porters seize and lift him*]   What news?[35] How now, masters?[36] What will ye do with me? Why do ye thus beset[37] me? Whither carry ye me? Help, help! Neighbors, friends, citizens!

MESSENIO   Oh, Jupiter, what do I see? My master abused by a company of varlets.

MENAECHMUS THE CITIZEN   Is there no good man will help me?

MESSENIO [*coming to the rescue*]   Help ye, master? Yes, the villains shall have my life before they shall thus wrong ye. 'Tis more fit I

32 **pricked** spurred   33 **basted** beaten   34 **fardels** parcels   35 **What news?** i.e., What's going on?   36 **masters** i.e., sirs.   37 **beset** surround with hostile intent

should be killed than you thus handled. Pull out that rascal's eye that holds ye about the neck there. I'll clout these peasants. Out, ye rogue! Let go, ye varlet!

MENAECHMUS THE CITIZEN   I have hold of this villain's eye.

MESSENIO   Pull it out, and let the place appear in his head.[38] Away, ye cutthroat thieves! Ye murderers!

ALL THE PORTERS   Oh, oh, ai, ai!   *Cry pitifully.**

MESSENIO   Away! Get ye hence, ye mongrels, ye dogs. [*Some flee.*] Will ye be gone? Thou rascal behind there, I'll give thee somewhat more. [*He attacks a straggler.*] Take that.   [*All disappear.*] It was time to come, master; you had been in good case[39] if I had not been here now. I told you what would come of it.

MENAECHMUS THE CITIZEN   Now, as the gods love me, my good friend, I thank thee. Thou hast done that for me which I shall never be able to requite.[40]

MESSENIO   I'll tell ye how, sir: give me my freedom.

MENAECHMUS THE CITIZEN   Should I give it thee?

MESSENIO   Seeing you cannot requite my good turn.

MENAECHMUS THE CITIZEN   Thou art deceived, man.

MESSENIO   Wherein?

MENAECHMUS THE CITIZEN   On mine honesty, I am none of thy master.[41] I had never yet any servant would do so much for me.

MESSENIO   Why, then, bid me be free. Will you?

MENAECHMUS THE CITIZEN   Yea, surely. Be free, for my part.

MESSENIO   Oh, sweetly spoken! Thanks, my good master. [*To himself*]* Messenio, we are all glad of your good fortune.

MESSENIO   Oh, master—I'll call ye master still—I pray, use me in any service as ye did before; I'll dwell with you still, and when ye go home I'll wait upon you.

MENAECHMUS THE CITIZEN   Nay, nay, it shall not need.

MESSENIO   I'll go straight to the inn and deliver up my accounts and all your stuff. Your purse is locked up safely sealed in the casket, as you gave it me. I will go fetch it to you.

MENAECHMUS THE CITIZEN   Do, fetch it.

MESSENIO   I will.   [*Exit.*]

---

38 let . . . head i.e., leave an empty eye socket.   **39 you . . . case** i.e., you would have been in a fine fix   **40 requite** repay.   **41 none . . . master** no master of yours.

MENAECHMUS THE CITIZEN   I was never thus perplexed. Some deny
me to be him that I am and shut me out of their doors. This fellow saith he is my bondman, and of me he begs his freedom. He
will fetch my purse and money. Well, if he bring it, I will receive
it and set him free. I would he would, so he* go his way. My old
father-in-law and the Doctor say I am mad. Whoever saw such
strange demeanors? Well, though Erotium be never so angry, yet
once again I'll go see if by entreaty I can get the cloak of* her to
carry to my wife.   *Exit [to the Courtesan's]*.

Enter Menaechmus the Traveler, and Messenio.

MENAECHMUS THE TRAVELER   Impudent knave, wilt thou say that I
ever saw thee since I sent thee away today and bade thee come
for me after dinner?

MESSENIO   Ye make me stark mad! I took ye away and rescued ye
from four great big-boned villains that were carrying ye away
even here in this place. Here they had ye up. You cried, "Help,
help!" I came running to you. You and I together beat them
away by main force. Then, for my good turn and faithful service,
ye gave me my freedom. I told ye I would go fetch your casket.
Now in the meantime you ran some other way to get before
me, and so you deny it all again.

MENAECHMUS THE TRAVELER   I gave thee thy freedom?

MESSENIO   You did.

MENAECHMUS THE TRAVELER   When I give thee thy freedom, I'll be
a bondman myself. Go thy ways.[42]

MESSENIO   Whew! Marry, I thank ye for nothing.

Enter Menaechmus the Citizen.

MENAECHMUS THE CITIZEN   [*calling back into the Courtesan's house*]
Forsworn queans,[43] swear till your hearts ache and your eyes fall
out! Ye shall never make me believe that I carried hence either
cloak or chain.

MESSENIO   [*to Menaechmus the Traveler*]   Oh, heavens, master, what
do I see?

_____

42 **Go thy ways** Get along with you.   43 **Forsworn queans** Lying
whores

MENAECHMUS THE TRAVELER What?

MESSENIO Your ghost.

MENAECHMUS THE TRAVELER What ghost?

MESSENIO Your image, as like you as can be possible.

MENAECHMUS THE TRAVELER Surely not much unlike me, as I think.

MENAECHMUS THE CITIZEN [*seeing Messenio*] O my good friend and helper, well met! Thanks for thy late good help.

MESSENIO Sir, may I crave to know your name?

MENAECHMUS THE CITIZEN I were too blame[44] if I should not tell thee anything. My name is Menaechmus.

MENAECHMUS THE TRAVELER Nay, my friend, that is my name.

MENAECHMUS THE CITIZEN I am of Syracuse in Sicily.

MENAECHMUS THE TRAVELER So am I.

MESSENIO [*to Menaechmus the Citizen*] Are you a Syracusan?

MENAECHMUS THE CITIZEN I am.

MESSENIO Oho, I know ye! This [*indicating the Citizen*] is my master; I thought he there had been my master, and was proffering my service to him. Pray pardon me, sir, if I said anything I should not.

MENAECHMUS THE TRAVELER Why, doting patch,[45] didst thou not come with me this morning from the ship?

MESSENIO My faith, he says true. This [*indicating the Traveler*] is my master; you may go look ye a man.—God save ye, master!—You, sir, farewell. This is Menaechmus.

MENAECHMUS THE CITIZEN I say that I am Menaechmus.

MESSENIO What a jest is this! Are you Menaechmus?

MENAECHMUS THE CITIZEN Even Menaechmus, the son of Moschus.

MENAECHMUS THE TRAVELER My father's son?

MENAECHMUS THE CITIZEN Friend, I go about neither to take your father nor your country from you.

MESSENIO O immortal gods, let it fall out as I hope! And, for my life, these are the two twins, all things agree so jump[46] together. I will speak to my master.—Menaechmus?

BOTH What wilt thou?

---

44 too blame exceedingly blameworthy **45 doting patch** foolish clown **46 jump** precisely

MESSENIO I call ye not both. But which of you came with me from the ship?

MENAECHMUS THE CITIZEN Not I.

MENAECHMUS THE TRAVELER I did.

MESSENIO Then I call you. Come hither.

                    [He takes Menaechmus the Traveler aside.]

MENAECHMUS THE TRAVELER What's the matter?

MESSENIO This same is either some notable cozening juggler or else it is your brother whom we seek. I never saw one man so like another. Water to water nor milk to milk is not liker than he is to you.

MENAECHMUS THE TRAVELER Indeed, I think thou say'st true. Find it that he is my brother, and I here promise thee thy freedom.

MESSENIO Well, let me about it. *[He takes Menaechmus the Citizen aside.]* Hear ye, sir, you say your name is Menaechmus?

MENAECHMUS THE CITIZEN I do.

MESSENIO So is this man's. You are of Syracuse?

MENAECHMUS THE CITIZEN True.

MESSENIO So is he. Moschus was your father?

MENAECHMUS THE CITIZEN He was.

MESSENIO So was he his. What will you say if I find that ye are brethren and twins?

MENAECHMUS THE CITIZEN I would think it happy news.

MESSENIO Nay, stay, masters both. I mean to have the honor of this exploit. Answer me: your name is Menaechmus?

MENAECHMUS THE CITIZEN Yea.

MESSENIO And yours?

MENAECHMUS THE TRAVELER And mine.

MESSENIO You are of Syracuse?

MENAECHMUS THE CITIZEN I am.

MENAECHMUS THE TRAVELER And I.

MESSENIO Well, this goeth right thus far. What is the farthest[47] thing that you remember there?

MENAECHMUS THE CITIZEN How I went with my father to Tarentum, to a great mart,[48] and there in the press[49] I was stolen from him.

---

47 farthest i.e., furthest back in time   **48 mart** market, fair   **49 press** crowd

MENAECHMUS THE TRAVELER Oh, Jupiter!

MESSENIO Peace, what exclaiming is this?—How old were ye then?

MENAECHMUS THE CITIZEN About seven year old, for even then I shed teeth;[50] and since that time I never heard of any of my kindred.

MESSENIO Had ye never a brother?

MENAECHMUS THE CITIZEN Yes, as I remember I heard them say we were two twins.

MENAECHMUS THE TRAVELER Oh, Fortune!

MESSENIO Tush, can ye not be quiet?—Were ye both of one name?

MENAECHMUS THE CITIZEN Nay, as I think, they called my brother Sosicles.

MENAECHMUS THE TRAVELER It is he. What need farther proof? Oh, brother, brother, let me embrace thee!

MENAECHMUS THE CITIZEN Sir, if this be true I am wonderfully glad. But how is it that ye are called Menaechmus?

MENAECHMUS THE TRAVELER When it was told us that you and our father were both dead, our grandsire, in memory of my father's name, changed mine to Menaechmus.

MENAECHMUS THE CITIZEN 'Tis very like[51] he would do so, indeed. But let me ask ye one question more: what was our mother's name?

MENAECHMUS THE TRAVELER Theusimarche.

MENAECHMUS THE CITIZEN Brother, the most welcome man to me that the world holdeth!

MENAECHMUS THE TRAVELER Ay, joy, and ten thousand joys the more, having taken so long travail and huge pains to seek you.

MESSENIO See now how all this matter comes about. This it was [indicating Menaechmus the Traveler] that the gentlewoman had ye in to dinner, thinking it had been he.

MENAECHMUS THE CITIZEN True it is, I willed a dinner to be provided for me here this morning, and I also brought hither closely[52] a cloak of my wife's and gave it to this woman.

MENAECHMUS THE TRAVELER [producing the cloak] Is not this the same, brother?

MENAECHMUS THE CITIZEN How came you by this?

50 shed teeth i.e., lost baby teeth 51 like likely 52 closely secretly

MENAECHMUS THE TRAVELER   This woman met me, had me into dinner, entertained me most kindly, and gave me this cloak and this chain. [*He shows the chain.*]

MENAECHMUS THE CITIZEN   Indeed, she took ye for me, and I believe I have been as strangely handled by occasion of your coming.

MESSENIO   You shall have time enough to laugh at all these matters hereafter. Do ye remember, master, what ye promised me?

MENAECHMUS THE CITIZEN   Brother, I will entreat you to perform your promise to Messenio. He is worthy of it.

MENAECHMUS THE TRAVELER   I am content.

MESSENIO   Io,[53] triumph!

MENAECHMUS THE TRAVELER   Brother, will ye now go with me to Syracuse?

MENAECHMUS THE CITIZEN   So soon as I can sell away such goods as I possess here in Epidamnum, I will go with you.

MENAECHMUS THE TRAVELER   Thanks, my good brother.

MENAECHMUS THE CITIZEN   Messenio, play thou the crier for me and make a proclamation.

MESSENIO   A fit office. Come on. Oyez! What day shall your sale be?

MENAECHMUS THE CITIZEN   This day sennight.[54]

MESSENIO [*making proclamation*]   All men, women, and children in Epidamnum or elsewhere that will repair to Menaechmus' house this day sennight shall there find all manner of things to sell:[55] servants, household stuff, house, ground, and all, so they bring ready money.—Will ye sell your wife too, sir?

MENAECHMUS THE CITIZEN   Yea, but I think nobody will bid money for her.

MESSENIO [*as Epilogue*]   Thus, gentlemen, we take our leaves, and if we have pleased, we require a *Plaudite*.[56]   [*Exeunt.*]

Text based on *Menaechmi. A Pleasant and Fine Conceited Comedy, Taken out of the Most Excellent Witty Poet, Plautus. . . . Written in English by W. W. . . . Printed by Tho. Creede. . . . 1595.*

---

53 **Io** (An exclamation of joy.)   54 **This day sennight** One week from now.   55 **to sell** on sale   56 **require a *Plaudite*** request applause at the end of the play.

In the following, departures from the original text appear in boldface;
original readings are in roman. Speech prefixes have been silently
regularized.

p. 165 *the the the   p. 167 *belongs belong   p. 169 [and
elsewhere] *Syracuse Syracusis   p. 170 *of off   p. 172 s.p.
*MENAECHMUS THE TRAVELER Pen   p. 175 *ails aile [also 20 lines
lower on p. 175]   p. 178 *come in come it   p. 182 *Jove Iobe
p. 187 *he [not in 1595]   p. 188 *s.d. Cry pitifully [included as part
of spoken text in 1595]   p. 188 *[To himself] [1595 here has a s.p.,
"Seruus Alius"]   p. 189 *he [not in 1595]   *of on

FURTHER READING

❦

Arthos, John. "Shakespeare's Transformation of Plautus." *Comparative Drama* 1 (1967–1968): 239–253. Rpt. and rev. in *Shakespeare: The Early Writings*. London: Bowes and Bowes, 1972. In a sustained analysis of Plautus, Arthos finds aspects in addition to farce that were resources for Shakespeare's transformation of the *Menaechmi*. In *The Comedy of Errors*, Shakespeare also exploits the "musicality" and "exuberance" of Plautus's art, heightening the Plautine emphasis on wonder and the power of love.

Baldwin, T. W. *On the Compositional Genetics of "The Comedy of Errors."* Urbana: Univ. of Illinois Press, 1965. Baldwin offers an exhaustive study of the background of Shakespeare's play. He discusses the play's structure, sources, and date in terms of the literary, intellectual, and political activity of England in the 1580s.

Barber, C. L. "Shakespearean Comedy in *The Comedy of Errors.*" *College English* 25 (1964): 493–497. Barber argues that the play transcends the outrageousness of its Roman model, framing the "animal or natural or foolish side of man by presentation of the normal and the ideal." The totality of Shakespeare's characterization, his testing and display of the bond of marriage, and his control of the "rhythm of feeling" serve to elevate the play above the farce of its source.

Berry, Ralph. "And Here We Wander in Illusions." *Shakespeare's Comedies: Explorations in Form*. Princeton, N.J.: Princeton Univ. Press, 1972. For Berry, the tragic frame and the psychological complexity of the characters work to graft onto the farce of *The Comedy of Errors* the serious thematic concerns of the later comedies. Out of the errors of farcical action emerges a comedy that explores the problems of human identity.

Brooks, Harold F. "Themes and Structure in *The Comedy of Errors.*" *Early Shakespeare*, ed. John Russell Brown and Bernard Harris. Stratford-upon-Avon Studies 3. London: Edward Arnold, 1961. Rpt. in *Shakespeare, the Comedies: A Collection of Critical*

Essays, ed. Kenneth Muir. Englewood Cliffs, N.J.: Prentice-Hall, 1965. Brooks discovers the play's richness in its complex structure, which "by parallel, contrast, or cross-reference . . . makes us compare one passage or person of the play with another." These juxtapositions organize the play's serious concerns with time and timing, order and illusion, into a dramatic whole that has the achievement of proper relationships at its center.

Elliott, G. R. "Weirdness in *The Comedy of Errors.*" *University of Toronto Quarterly* 9 (1939): 95–106. The psychological horror of the suggestion of dual identity, the "strange" tones of romance, and the play's subtle sounding of pathos all combine to shed what Elliott describes as a "ray of weird light, romantic and comic . . . upon *The Comedy of Errors.*"

Freedman, Barbara. "Egeon's Debt: Self-Division and Self-Redemption in *The Comedy of Errors.*" *English Literary Renaissance* 10 (1980): 360–383. Freedman argues for the play's integrated structure: the frame of Egeon's redemption is filled and resolved by the activity in Ephesus, which is the site of a "carefully orchestrated psychological drama in which disassociated parts of the self are meaningfully united."

Hamilton, A. C. "The Early Comedies: *The Comedy of Errors.*" *The Early Shakespeare*. San Marino, Calif.: Huntington Library, 1967. For Hamilton, plot is the primary concern of the play: Shakespeare reshapes the mechanics of the Plautine comedy by doubling its twins, relocating its setting, and infusing a note of madness and nightmare into the simple comedy of mistaken identities. The result is a play in which the restoration of stable identities at the end is a significant assertion of the logic of the comic form.

Kinney, Arthur F. "Staging *The Comedy of Errors.*" *Shakespeare: Text and Theater: Essays in Honor of Jay L. Halio*, ed. Lois Potter and Arthur F. Kinney. Newark, Del.: Univ. of Delaware Press, 1999. Using *The Comedy of Errors* as a test case, Kinney explores the question of where the meaning of play text lies: in the script or in performance. Looking at the various interpretations of the play that have succeeded on stage, Kinney argues for "the synergy of text and performance": the provocations of the written text and the willingness of individual productions selectively to illuminate any of these.

Leggatt, Alexander. *"The Comedy of Errors." Shakespeare's Comedy of Love*. London: Methuen; New York: Barnes and Noble, 1974. Leggatt argues that underlying the play's "farcical comedy of situation" is a subtler comedy of character. The play's confusions of identity and collisions of dramatic styles permit an examination of the difficulties of fully knowing and understanding ourselves or others, difficulties that are resolved in the restoration of the family unit at the end.

Miola, Robert S., ed. *"The Comedy of Errors": Critical Essays*. New York and London: Garland, 1997. Miola's anthology offers an extremely useful collection of materials, including his own overview of the critical reception of the play, a generous selection of the major scholarly studies (including work by Baldwin, Brooks, Freedman, and Leggatt listed here), some new work on the play and its performance history (including pieces by Arthur Kinney, Douglas Lanier, and Joseph Candido), and reviews of various productions.

Nevo, Ruth. "My Glass and Not My Brother." *Comic Transformations in Shakespeare*. London and New York: Methuen, 1980. The role-playing demanded by the farce of *The Comedy of Errors* is, according to Nevo, therapeutic for the characters: "fooled, they become, to whatever degree, aware of themselves as selves and as fooled, and so have a basis for the regaining of control." In its concern with the discovery of identity, *The Comedy of Errors* reveals its strong affinities with Shakespeare's later comedies.

Parker, Patricia. "The Bible and the Marketplace: *The Comedy of Errors*." *Shakespeare from the Margins: Language, Culture, Context*. Chicago and London: Univ. of Chicago Press, 1996. With her characteristically patient attention to the linguistic densities of a text, Parker explores the largely unexamined concentration of biblical fragments and allusions that marks *The Comedy of Errors*. Parker shows how this material demonstrates how much more the play is than the inconsequential farce it is often played as, and then locates the issues raised within a wider context of "Shakespearean stagings of biblical reference."

Perry, Curtis. "Commerce, Community, and Nostalgia in *The Comedy of Errors*." *Money and the Age of Shakespeare: Essays in New Economic Criticism*, ed. Linda Woodbridge. London: Palgrave, 2003. In an alert and sophisticated essay, Perry focuses on the play's preoccupation with money and commercial goods, and finds in this an economic basis for the play's wider concern with the tensions between the isolated individual and the bonds of community.

Salgādo, Gāmini. " 'Time's Deformed Hand': Sequence, Consequence, and Inconsequence in *The Comedy of Errors.*" *Shakespeare Survey* 25 (1972): 81–91. Salgādo sees the play's preoccupation with time as a function of its concern with identity. The play's farcical duplications of identity apparently distort time and disrupt the logic of cause and effect, but the play's design "is essentially benevolent," leading to a conclusion in which "all disorders are healed and all divisions settled."

Salingar, Leo. *Shakespeare and the Traditions of Comedy*, esp. pp. 59–67. Cambridge: Cambridge Univ. Press, 1974. Salingar discusses the play in terms of its relation to classical and medieval prose romance, and offers, among others, *Apollonius of Tyre* and the legends of Saint Clement and Saint Eustace as possible influences upon the play's construction.

MEMORABLE LINES

❧

Every why hath a wherefore.   (S. DROMIO 2.2.43–4)

What he hath scanted men in hair he hath given them in wit.
                                               (S. DROMIO 2.2.79–80)

Am I in earth, in heaven, or in hell?
Sleeping or waking, mad or well-advised?
                                               (S. ANTIPHOLUS 2.2.211–12)

There is something in the wind.   (E. ANTIPHOLUS 3.1.69)

For slander lives upon succession,
Forever housèd where it gets possession.
                                               (BALTHASAR 3.1.105–6)

A back friend, a shoulder clapper.   (S. DROMIO 4.2.37)

. . . one Pinch, a hungry, lean-faced villain,
A mere anatomy, a mountebank,
A threadbare juggler and a fortune-teller,
A needy, hollow-eyed, sharp-looking wretch,
A living dead man.   (E. ANTIPHOLUS 5.1.238–42)

I think you all have drunk of Circe's cup.   (DUKE 5.1.271)

After so long grief, such nativity!   (ABBESS 5.1.407)

SEE YOUR BOOKSELLER FOR THESE BANTAM CLASSICS

EARLY AFRICAN-AMERICAN CLASSICS, 0-553-21379-2
FIFTY GREAT SHORT STORIES, 0-553-27745-6
FIFTY GREAT AMERICAN SHORT STORIES, 0-553-27294-2
SHORT SHORTS, 0-553-27440-6
GREAT AMERICAN SHORT STORIES, 0-440-33060-2
SHORT STORY MASTERPIECES, 0-440-37864-8
THE VOICE THAT IS GREAT WITHIN US, 0-553-26263-7
THE BLACK POETS, 0-553-27563-1
THREE CENTURIES OF AMERICAN POETRY, (Trade) 0-553-37518-0,
    (Hardcover) 0-553-10250-8